I0410099

First published in Ebook and Paperback form in 2023
Copyright © Peter Joe Hulmes, 2023

—^^—

The right of Peter Joe Hulmes to be identified as the author
of this work has been asserted in accordance with the
Copyright, Designs and Patents Act, 1988.

unijuve@yahoo.com

—^^—

The author and publishers have made all reasonable efforts
to contact copyright-holders for permission, and apologise
for any omissions or errors in the form of credits given.
Corrections may be made to future printings.

—^^—

ISBN: 9798864078976
A digital version of this book is available on
amazon.co.uk and other territories.

universal juvenile

in search of Kim Mitchell

PETER JOE HULMES

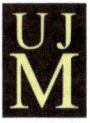

In memoriam

James & Marjorie Hulmes (1931 - 2016)
Sharon Tracey Hulmes (1964 - 2012)

about the author

(And about the Book!)

Peter Joe Hulmes is a Husband, Father, Grandfather, Carpenter, retired Policeman, songwriter and habitual singer of songs. I can't claim to be his friend. We only met in 2023 but I knew him by email as long ago as 2010 when I came across the quite excellent CD his band Universal Juveniles had produced as a tribute to an obscure (for some) 1970's Canadian rock band, Max Webster (If you haven't heard the CD, pretty much anyone connected with this book will happily get one in your hands!).

During email communications with Pete and his friend Mick Wilson, I discovered they had visited Canada to see the Max Webster singer and guitarist, Kim Mitchell perform live and had many Max Webster related adventures. Mick casually mentioned that Pete had written a journal of their experiences. I was intrigued and wanted to see it and read it as I too, was a fan of Kim Mitchell and his former band Max Webster. Pete was reluctant as it was not finished or ready for sharing etc. and slowly, we dropped out of communication.

That was until the launch of the amazing forensic study in book form of Max Webster's career by the Guitarist, Archivist and Author, Bob Wegner. A staggering piece of work which instigated me getting back in touch with Pete and Mick to share information about the book 'High Class' by Bob.

Of course, I hadn't forgotten about the journal mentioned over ten years ago. Did he still have it? Eventually, the answer was yes! I offered to edit it for him and he agreed! so I soon got his paper notes and a digital copy transcribed by his daughter Leigh-Anne.

I had never before edited a book but I had experience in communications in the corporate world. How hard could it be? Besides, I wanted to read it and see it published to the world and the many Max Webster fans out there.

The book covers much of Pete's adult life but mostly when he travelled to, worked and lived for extended periods in Canada and fell in love with the country, its culture and people. But at it's core, it tells of his somewhat delayed discovery of Kim Mitchell and Max Webster and how he came to love their music above many other artists. A bold statement because the other thing about Pete is how big a music fan he is, with a broad eclectic taste and a lifetime of seeing bands at their best in the live environment.

If you enjoy this book half as much as I did, I will have contributed my time to a worthwhile project.

Bob Holt, Editor
book@bobholt.uk

foreword

This is a story of incredible coincidences and fortuitous encounters. It's a story of obsession, passion, drive and desire. Above all, it is a tale of one man's love of another man's music and how that passion resulted in a life-long journey to meet and emulate a hero.

It's also a story of setbacks, hardships, trials and tribulations. Not least of which was the day I switched on my computer to find 161 pages of the manuscript for this book, the entire thing at that stage, had vanished. Disappeared. I was inconsolable, as I knew that my little project, my dream, was well and truly over.

Discussing this tragedy with my daughter later, she informed me that two weeks earlier, for no apparent reason, she had transcribed the entire manuscript to disc! I say again, there was no request or reason for her to have performed that miraculous act. I am forever in her debt.

During the journey in the story, I develop life-long friendships, some of them spanning two continents. I fall in love with the home country of the musician featured in the book (Canada and Kim Mitchell respectively) and I find true, personal love and salvation.

All of this eventually culminating in a joyous celebration of life, art and euphoric realisation. The whole journey, despite the setbacks, was an absolute pleasure.

I sincerely hope you enjoy it.

Peter Joe Hulmes.
unijuve@yahoo.com

Chapters

easy to shame

"Shooting stars fly higher than the moon, Reality? It's just a cartoon!"

Lyrics taken from 'Higher Than the Moon
(Caught in the Web)' by The Universal Juveniles (Hulmes / Oldale)

I was born in Crumpsall, Manchester, England in 1962. A million miles away from Sarnia in Ontario, Canada where ten years previously, an amazing musician was born. Someone who would become very important to the musical landscape of my life; Kim Mitchell.

I hate to admit it, but awareness of Kim Mitchell (Singer, guitarist and songwriter for Max Webster) completely passed me by until 1986, which was an incredible eleven years after the release of Max Websters' eponymous debut album and an astonishing six years after their untimely demise. Even more bewildering as I was a huge music fan from the tender age of eleven and I fell in love with Roxy Music, Cockney Rebel, Sparks and other similar bands that were… Quirky? They would certainly sit alongside Max Webster very well!

My love of music led on to me becoming a singer in local bar bands from 1978 to the present. I sang the usual fare for a rock fan growing up in 1970s England, UFO, Thin Lizzy, Judas Priest, Queen etc. but still knowledge of the mighty Max Webster eluded me.

Returning to my childhood, I was six when my family moved from Manchester to the small town of Clitheroe in the Ribble Valley area. A distance of only 24 miles by car, but a million miles in terms of culture, music and anything bordering cool but I was young so I didn't quite feel the culture shock as much as my older brothers. Clitheroe was a wonderful place to grow up and I loved my childhood but if I'd had any chance of being introduced to the music of Max Webster and Kim Mitchell, that would have probably have been back in Manchester. Clitheroe, to my mind, had barely heard of the Beatles, let alone much else.

Growing up, I became involved in music quite obsessively; brothers and friends record collections, radio, TV, (all three English channels), books and magazines, and then eventually meeting and joining musicians with similar and varied tastes, but still, not a single mention of Max Webster.

A few Canadian artists did seep through though, and I picked up on Triumph, Saga, Neil Young, Loverboy and of course Rush, but not many more. I've always thought that Canadian music had a rough time in the UK music press over the years. Unjustly slagged off, or just completely ignored.

I became a Rush fan around 1978 after a film clip of them performing Xanadu was shown on the seminal BBC music program 'The Old Grey Whistle Test', essential viewing for every 'muso' during its 25-year run. I managed to see Rush live for the first time at the back end of 1979. They had completed their Hemispheres European tour earlier in the year but did a smaller tour late summer which saw them play the only two European tour dates in Bingley Hall, Stafford supported by ex Thin Lizzy guitarist Brian Robertson's Wild Horses. I had not known at the time that Max Webster was the support for the Hemispheres tour earlier in the year. This meant that I had missed Max Webster live by just a few short months.

While on the Hemispheres tour in the UK, Max Webster made an improbable, yet incredible appearance on the BBC's other musical institution 'Top of The Pops', performing 'Paradise Skies' from the Million Vacations album. Like the 'Whistle Test' show, I was an avid watcher of TOTP but I totally missed this broadcast! It appeared that things were conspiring against me ever coming across this band.

A further example of me not picking up on Max Webster was when they and Rush recorded a song called 'Battlescar!' together in 1980 and the song was released as a 7" single. I remember actually holding a copy of the record in my hands and I recall wondering what it was? But (and I know how insane this must sound) I didn't buy singles. I was an album guy. Always have been, always will be. So, I let this introduction to the band slip through my fingers and I still didn't know what I was missing.

Being a Rush fan introduced me to the genius of Pye Dubois long before I found Max Webster. He was the lyric writer for nearly all Max Webster songs and he co-wrote the lyrics on the mighty 'Tom Sawyer' from my personal favourite Rush album 'Moving Pictures'. He cropped up a few more times throughout Rush's career on the 'Hold Your Fire' track 'Force Ten', 'Between Sun & Moon' from the 'Counterparts' album, and the title track from 'Test for Echo'. For myself, I find these latter three tracks to be much better realised than 'Tom Sawyer'. All great tasters yet I was still to uncover the true majesty of his work alongside Kim Mitchell in Max Webster.

In 1981, I answered an advert in a local paper for a singer required for local heroes Oxym. They were part of the 'New Wave of British Heavy Metal' movement which bore bands such as Def Leppard, Iron Maiden, Saxon as well as many others. They were really a very good band, with unusual song structures, and great choruses and were very dynamic live. They had a very strong local following and definitely had the potential to be successful.

Unfortunately for me, they also had Rob Rigby, one of the area's best vocalists. Although I did the best I could, the band was never as good without Rob, and this version of the band didn't last long.

One thing I didn't know at the time was that their drummer, Michael Wilson, or 'Mik' as he liked to be known at the time, was a huge Max Webster fan. True to form (well, my form anyway) this was never mentioned, and when I left the band in '82, I still had not been introduced to the music of Kim Mitchell.

After leaving Oxym, I lost touch with Mick until 2001 when we bumped into each other at a friend's 40th birthday bash. It was great to see him again! We already had a shared love of Manchester City Football Club but as I had discovered Max Webster since we last saw each other, we now had this extra wonderful connection which would lead us to a very enjoyable and fruitful musical adventure! But that's for later...

"Check!! Check!!"

words to worse

I took my first visit to Canada in 1983. A very good friend of mine, Andrew 'Wilko' Wilkinson, had family acquaintances living in Calgary and he was planning to visit them as part of a two-month trip. Wilko was not only a good friend but also a very gifted guitarist. We had worked together in a couple of bands before, and would work together in the future.

I invited myself on the Canada trip and we decided to fly to Toronto and then travel west to Alberta. We met someone on the plane and ended up spending our first few nights in action packed Sudbury, Ontario, of all places. It was all a strange new world to us and we had a ball. The things that stick in your mind: doughnuts for supper! What's all that about?

Next stop was Montreal where we met up with Rick Beckett, an old friend from back home in Clitheroe, who'd recently gone to live with his father in the LaSalle area.

It was very much a music trip and we saw a few bands on our travels. Styx at the Montreal Forum on the 'Kilroy Was Here' tour was a particular highlight. We listened endlessly to the great Canadian rock radio stations: Chum FM in Montreal, Q107 in Toronto, and we picked up on a few more artists new to us: Bryan Adams, Toronto, and Coney Hatch. I would learn later that the first Coney Hatch album was produced by Kim Mitchell(!!) but I was still a few years away from connecting to the music of my yet undiscovered hero.

One time we were browsing in a record store on Yonge Street, Toronto. We must have been talking and someone overheard us. "English mate?" asked a cockney accent. It was a guy from London (England, not Ontario), who introduced himself as Robert Plant's tour manager. We knew that Plant had played in Montreal a couple of nights earlier and was due to play out West and he explained that he was having a couple of days break before joining the tour. He showed us his tour pass and some other tour paraphernalia and we were mightily impressed. After a while he asked us if we'd eaten and he offered to by us lunch. We refused the lunch but said we'd share a drink with him. We crossed Yonge Street and went into the Nag's Head bar.

I remember him ordering the food and drinks as we sat at a table. He then enquired whether we used cash or had a credit card. Credit cards were a little new to us at the time so we told him cash. "You should always use credit cards," he said "cash is inconvenient. Cards are so much easier to use and carry and there's less risk of you losing or having your money stolen." or words to that effect. A few minutes later, armed police entered and arrested our friend for using a stolen credit card. Robert Plant's tour manager's stolen credit card.

We were taken to one side and questioned, while still in the Nag's Head, and luckily, they believed we'd only just met the guy and knew nothing of the theft. Now, as if all this wasn't bad enough, as they handcuffed him and began to take him away, I noticed he'd left his cigarettes on the table. I asked him if he wanted them and he said yes and turned his body slightly so I could place them in his pocket. As I reached for his pocket with the cigarettes the police officer panicked and pulled his fucking gun on me!! Now, you have to remember that we didn't (and still don't) have armed police in England, so the sight of the gun in its holster was one thing, but when it was out and pointed at me, I nearly shat myself. Talk about things going from bad to worse.

A couple of weeks later, I said my farewells to Canada and Wilko as I left him in Calgary and flew home. Wilko stayed on for another month to travel up to Edmonton.

I'd spent a month in Canada, stopping in Sudbury, Montreal, Toronto, Thunder Bay and finally, Calgary. I fell in love with the country and its people and vowed to return. Also, its music was beginning to prick my interest and seep into my subconscious. I had picked up a various artists album to bring home called 'Electric North'. An excellent compilation, featuring mainly new material from bands like Chilliwack, Toronto, Sheriff and Coney Hatch (but no Kim Mitchell!). Despite living in the country for a month, I still had no idea of the existence of Max Webster or Kim Mitchell, or how the discovery of them would affect my life so dramatically in the future.

Upon my return to England, my life continued as normal. The band I was in at the time - Tokyo - had some interested parties and at one point we auditioned for a company that was looking for bands to perform in Abu Dhabi of all places, for the British oil workers over there. It turned out that the whole thing was a bit too 'cabaret' for us and the trip never came off. The company really liked us though and were interested enough to pay for us to record four original songs in a studio in a place called Newton-le-Willows, not too far from home. One of the tracks, a song called 'Soliloquy', I wrote during the Canadian trip and was originally called... wait for it... 'North Bay Blues'. How poor was that title? I suppose you can guess where that was written - at three in the morning in a coffee shop waiting for the earliest bus to take us to Thunder Bay:

"I've seen the desserts, I've seen the falls,
I've seen the cities, I've seen it all,
But through all these wonders`, I still recall,
The memories of home."

Lyrics from 'Soliloquy' by Tokyo (Hulmes/Ellis/Dickinson/Cowgill/Spalding)

It was a long night! We sent the demo to a few companies but nothing ever came of it.

As far as my pre-Max/Mitchell days go, that's about it. I was a huge music fan with a varied taste. Although I knew there was obviously some great new music to come, I believed that I'd absorbed everything good that was already out there, and that nothing new was going to excite me in the same way as, say, Roxy Music had way back in 1972. Little did I know that my favourite band and musicians of all time had already been in existence for ten years or more.

I didn't know it at the time, but I would soon be "Shaking like a Human Being".

april in toronto

By 1986 things had become a little stale for me back home. I don't quite know how it had happened but I found myself singing as part of a boy/girl cabaret duo called Jupiter. We were using one of the very first Karaoke machines. We had a lot of work, but I knew deep down that we were not good and that this was not what I wanted to be doing.

Around this time, I had a surprise visit from my very good friend Rick from Montreal who was back in the UK visiting family. He tried to be complimentary to what I was doing musically, but I could see in his eyes he wondered what the hell I was doing. He liked his music loud and proud and we were not that. I decided I couldn't continue with Jupiter and this planted a seed in my mind about returning to Canada.

Rick's father had moved from Montreal to Toronto for work reasons and although Rick was currently still living in LaSalle, sleeping on friends' floors, he said he would probably follow his father to Toronto as there seemed to be more work prospects there. This inspired me to return to Canada and when Rick left to return home, I told him I would join him as soon as I had raised enough cash to fund an extended stay.

By March '86, I was ready. I had left 'Jupiter' and sold nearly everything I owned. One of the few things I didn't sell was my record collection, which numbered around two thousand by this time. My mother and father kindly agreed to house these for me until I returned.

Record collections are such a wonderful thing. When you come across a serious collection, I think it reads almost like a personal diary or memoir. The collector can tell you so much about themselves, based on the records in the collection. Where they were at certain times in their lives, and even where their head was at when they bought that Johnny Cash album or that Bay City Rollers record. As a Rock Music fan, there were quite a few guilty secrets tucked away in my collection: A-ha lying next to AC/DC, Dean Friedman side by side with The Fixx, K. D. Lang neighbours with Led Zeppelin, but I wouldn't change any of it. Not a thing.

This was it then. The flight was booked. Friday 13th April 1986. An unfortunate date I know, but I've never been superstitious.

I arrived at Pearson International Airport and somehow missed my ride to my destination. Rick had arranged to pick me up but couldn't find me? Overslept and hungover more like... I caught the bus to downtown instead and it was a blessing in disguise. I could see the city in the distance and as it slowly drew near, I was able to soak in its full majesty. I've visited more than a few cities over the years, London, Glasgow, Brussels, Paris, New York, Calgary, but I can tell you that Toronto's skyline is definitely the most impressive, especially from the lake. Not as dramatic as say Manhattan, but it appears to have more structure and planning to it, not 'hap-hazard' like most cities. A wonderful sight.

The bus drove over the Gardiner expressway and I had fantastic views of both Toronto city centre and Lake Ontario. I was tingling with nervous excitement, full of anticipation and optimism. The sky was a brilliant deep blue. The whole future looked fantastically bright, as bright as the landscape before me. Although it had only been three years since I was last here, it felt like a lifetime of waiting was finally over. I had come home. I welled up and had to fight back an uncharacteristic tear as the situation began to overwhelm me (that explains the K.D. Lang records then!).

I had really landed on my feet coming back to Canada. Rick and his dad were living on Glen Manor Drive right in the 'Beaches' area just three properties up from the lake itself. This was going to be my home for as long as I wanted. Ain't life amazing?!

The Beaches area just blew me away. I couldn't have scripted it any better if I'd written it myself. I was one minute from early morning or late-night walks along the boulevard, which also offered fantastic views of Toronto's skyline across the water. The apartment was spacious and full of laughter, beer (lager and ale, naturally), and music. Queen street East was a hive of activity. Funky shops, including record shops, coffee houses, great bars, and a park (Kew Gardens). All in all, a really laid-back atmosphere with cool and friendly people. An idyllic location for anyone, especially a budding musician.

There was music everywhere in the Beaches: live bands most evenings during the summer, bands in the park and great music being played in the bars and discos. I discovered most Canadians of a certain age believe that England was responsible for much of the great music over the years, and it is hard to deny when you think of the Rolling Stones, The Beatles, Led Zeppelin, Yes, Elton John and even in the eighties with Duran Duran and Def Leppard.

But English radio and to a certain extent TV, was controlled by the BBC (the British Broadcasting Corporation) and you really struggled to hear anything other than the current favourite 'bubble-gum' rubbish that was deemed suitable for us to hear. This went for Scotland, Wales and Northern Ireland as well. We should never forget that The Sex Pistols' 'God Save The Queen' was number one in the charts in Britain but not played on the BBC. Rod Stewart at number two with 'I Don't Wanna Talk About It' was the 'official' number one despite being out sold by the Pistols, reportedly, by a hundred to one.

Rock music was rarely played on mainstream radio in England, except on specialist, one-hour programmes, once a week and usually after midnight. And this has only just begun to change with the introduction of digital radio via the Internet. I can even listen to Toronto Q107 in my living room in Lancashire; especially the Kim Mitchell show which broadcasts from 7pm GMT.

Canadian radio and its clubs were dominated by rock music in the '80s. It also seemed to be the average person on the streets' choice as well. It was a rock fan's paradise and as music was central to my life, the availability and accessibility of great music in Canada was a key reason why I was to return there many, many times.

I'd put you "here in my shoes", indeed.

water me drown

I managed to secure myself some work helping to renovate and convert an old church into a night club for teenagers. I'm a qualified carpenter having passed my exams back in 1982. The church conversion was situated in the upper Beaches area on Kingston Road. We were only a small workforce and the job wasn't well funded as the investor wanted to spend as little as possible, so it seemed to take forever.

I've visited the area more recently and sadly, the old building is no longer there having been replaced by an apartment block. It did open though, but I was told it wasn't very successful and didn't stay open long. I'm glad it wasn't condemned based on my building work!

The work crew were a good bunch and I was invited to different homes on occasion for certain functions. One of those occasions was for the opening ceremony of the '86 FIFA World Cup which was held in Mexico that year. It was the year of 'the Hand of God' incident whereby a well-known Argentinian footballer scored a winning goal against England off his hand. Seen by all except the referee…

Another workmate Edward 'Ted' Shay would play a pivotal role in my discovery of Max Webster and Kim Mitchell in the not-too-distant future. He will forever have my gratitude and I shall remain forever in his debt. Although he doesn't know that, so don't tell him.

Wide eyed, I continued to soak up the new experiences which continually came my way in this great city, province and country. This isn't a 'travelogue' so I won't list all the new experiences except perhaps for Niagara Falls. It is breath-taking. Everyone should experience the 'maid of the mist'. It's the perfect way to take in this wonder of the natural world.

Man-made wonders also abound aplenty. I'm sure my neck has never been the same since I first stood at its base and gazed up at the colossal majesty of the CN tower: the tallest free-standing structure in the world. As magnificent to view from outside as the views from its observation decks.

I watched baseball live for the first time at the Exhibition Centre (Ex). The Blue Jays. A fantastic experience, but, I'm sorry to all baseball fans. I went a few times, but I just couldn't get into it. Not enough happens for me until near the end. Cricket fans don't mind it apparently. It must be a 'stats' thing, as opposed to action. When I first met Kim Mitchell, I remember him saying, "You have to be drunk to watch baseball". How right he was.

I became a lifelong Argonauts fan during the '86 season though. Love the game. Maybe not as much as the NFL, but Toronto isn't in that so... Go CFL! I watched every home game that season. I got pissed wet through more times than I care to remember. The old stadium had no cover in the bleachers where I sat, as money was tight. The Argos got to the Eastern final that year, against their old rivals the Hamilton Tiger-cats.

They took a surprise lead from the first game back to the Ex. But, in the second game, they were their usual calamitous selves and threw the game away. Badly. They played as though they had never met each other before. It shouldn't have bothered me as much as it did, but I was gutted. Depressed for weeks. It reminded me so much of my repeated disappointments suffered through being a Manchester City fan, who's colours are also blue, that I decided it was fate and I've stuck with the Argos' ever since.

I don't wish to offend any purists out there, but I'm hoping Toronto get an NFL franchise sometime soon. I prefer the four downs, no points for a missed field goal, and shorter field/end zone. But hey... what do I know?

I also discovered hot chicken wings at Scratch Daniels famous half price nights in the Beaches. Chicken wings? Back in northern England in the early '80s the wings were one of the parts of the chicken we threw away. Now here was somebody that wanted to charge me good money to serve them to me in a restaurant? Delicious. I couldn't get enough of them. Of course, now, you can't move for wings on menus in England; North or South.

When I think back to the summer of 1986, I can only ever remember it being hot and every day having brilliant sunshine and clear blue skies, unlike our 'legendary' British summers of persistent rain and grey skies. We still talk about the glorious, heat-wave summer of 1976 as though we are lucky to be alive. But I know that my weather memory of Toronto '86 is wildly inaccurate. In fact, '86 was apparently Toronto's wettest summer for forty years. I found this out the hard way.

Back at the apartment on Glen Manor Drive I was living in the basement which, although only partially renovated, had a good bedroom area and was quite spacious. I obviously didn't have many possessions anyway, so I didn't need much space, just somewhere warm and dry.

What nobody mentioned to me was when it rains in southern Ontario, the lake rises! Now, you have to remember that we were only three properties up from the lake. A great spot, as I've said. But...

One evening I woke up in the middle of the night, around 2am I think. I didn't know what had woken me, I used to sleep like a rock right through to the alarm. Unlike now, when I'm lucky if I only have to get up three times to go and piss. But that's another story.

Anyway, there I was, lying in the pitch black wide awake. I thought I may as well go to the bathroom so I swung my legs out of the bed and onto the floor. If I hadn't been fully awake before, I bloody well was now! I was up to my knees in wet! Eyes wide, I dove for the 'lazy' switch above the bed and saw that I was sat in two feet of muddy, gurgling water which was sloshing all around me and the room.

"What the fuck? Are we sinking?" I thought I was going to drown. But, hang on a minute, I'm not even on a boat! My clothes and papers and things I couldn't even recognise were all floating and bobbing around the room. I was absolutely stunned. Eventually it dawned on me that I was actually sat in Lake Ontario. It was the most shocking way I have ever woken up. Funny though, eventually. I highly recommend it. Although it did take weeks to dry out all the furniture, and I ended up throwing some clothes and shoes away.

In hindsight, I suppose that from that moment on I should have used "borrowed shoes'".

radio for rock 'n' roll men

There was great music around that summer. Robert Palmer's 'Riptide' album, his 'Addicted to Love' single and iconic video were everywhere. I managed to see Palmer at the Forum in Ontario Place. An 'in-the-round' man made amphitheatre with a rotating stage. A superb venue situated right by the lake. It has since been replaced by the 'Molson Amphitheatre'.

 Two other acts I saw there that summer were 'Glass Tiger', who's album 'The Thin Red Line' became album of the year as I remember. A good album, although I don't think it has stood the test of time too well. I also fulfilled a lifetime ambition and managed to see the legendary 'Temptations'... Twice! Not only did I catch them at the Forum but also at the Roy Thomson Hall later in the year. What a wonderful time I was having.

The radio was full of fantastic new summer hits. 'Don't Forget Me When I'm Gone' by the aforementioned 'Glass Tiger', Gowan with 'Strange Animal'. Peter Gabriel's 'So', The Fixx with 'Walkabout'. I know that I've missed many more out, but it was a very good year for new music, especially for the radio.

I learned later of two fantastic debut albums that were released that year in England. 'The Broadcast' by the Cutting Crew and 'The Big Lad in The Windmill' by It Bites. A band that later reminded me a little of Max Webster. You should check them out.

It was, perhaps, the last truly good musical year for a long time. Despite, that is, for the emergence of 'The Tragically Hip' and the 'Rheostatics' the following year. Both superb Canadian national treasures.

A band I was already a fan of was 'Honeymoon Suite'. Their self-titled debut was a favourite of mine. I could never see what it was that Bon Jovi had that 'Honeymoon Suite' didn't have, apart from not being American that is. Their second album, 'The Big Prize' was a smash that summer. I think they had at least four songs from the album as singles. I managed to see them at Canada's Wonderland on a very cold, late summer (nearly autumn), evening. They were supported by Cats Can Fly, whom I quite liked. Guilty secrets again?

I went mad on concerts that year: The Moody Blues, The Fixx, twice, Peter Gabriel and Billy Joel, both at the Maple Leaf Gardens, Elton John at the Ex... I also visited smaller venues like the Gasworks downtown on Yonge Street; two floors of solid, loud rock with wall to wall 'rock-chicks'. Needless to say, I spent most Saturday nights there. It was 'manna from heaven' for us rock 'n' roll men. I was disappointed to discover it had closed its doors a few years ago. No doubt another victim of the burgeoning Karaoke and DJ crap-craze.

Due to parts of The Rolling Stones' 'Love You Live' album being recorded there; I also located and spent a couple of hours in the famous El Mocambo club on Spadina Avenue. To tell you the truth, I think I had actually gone for a Chinese meal at China Town and someone had mentioned that the club wasn't far away. I'm glad I went. I now have some major bragging rights amongst my fellow Stones fans.

As you can see, thanks to music (and chicken wings), I was really getting myself about. I was even helping tourists with directions when they were lost. Go figure!

In such a short time, I had seen, heard and partaken in a variety of what you might call Canadiana. Sadly, the variety excluded Max Webster and Kim Mitchell but Max Webster was still not on my radar, not yet anyway. But all that, and my musical perception, was about to change. Subtly, at first.

Sometime toward the end of July, Rick dropped the bombshell that he wasn't able to settle in Toronto and so he started making plans to return to Montreal. As this also coincided with Rick's father's girlfriend arriving to stay indefinitely, I decided that I didn't wish to cramp their style, and so moved out from Glen Manor myself.

I moved into a house share scenario on Woodbine Avenue, about halfway between Queen Street and Kingston Road, near to the old race track; something else that's no longer there. I was really sorry to be leaving such a wonderfully situated abode, but Woodbine Avenue wasn't too bad and the rent was reasonable.

My landlord, Frank, earned his living playing piano, by teaching, playing solo shows and also with a band called the Grandpa Band. He had two solo residences at two different venues on Danforth Avenue. I can't remember the names of the venues, but I sang at both of them on occasion, accompanied by Frank on the piano.

I had received news that my brother, Steven, was getting married in September. I didn't have the money to return home for the wedding but my boss at the church conversion job, Kirk, kindly and incredibly, offered to lend me the money as long as I returned to finish off the night club. I took him up on the offer and to help with the finances, I handed my accommodation notice in with Frank so that I could use the months rental deposit owed to me. Kirk offered me the use of his apartment in Crescent Town when I returned. This was a little too far from the Beaches for me, but I didn't want to appear ungrateful, so I accepted and flew home for a two-week holiday.

England was great! It felt like I had been away a lifetime. I crammed so much activity in, including the wedding, that I returned to Canada at the end of September burned out and in need of a rest. It was a good job I was on holiday. Boy, was I confused!

As the summer rolled on toward autumn, or, 'the fall' as it's known in North America and Canada, the church conversion was slowly beginning to take shape. I enjoyed the work, especially as it was giving me plenty of opportunity to listen to the radio. Q107 rock radio ruled!!

Through the summer I had begun to pick up on the odd song or three that I really began to like. It seemed that someone by the name of Kim Mitchell had a new album out? They were playing quite a few tracks from the album over and over again. You know what radio's like, whichever country it's in. Most songs get on your nerves after you've heard it four or five times in the last three hours. But, for me, these songs were different. 'Patio Lanterns', 'Alana Loves Me', 'Get Lucky (Boys and Girls)', 'That's The Hold', 'In My Shoes'... Wow!! This was fantastic music. Bright. Uplifting. The choruses were impeccable, as was the production and musicianship. And these tracks were all from one album? Unbelievable. Just my kind of thing.

Other tracks by this amazing, 'unknown', artist were being requested by other listeners and I was treated to other 'first-time' gems like 'Go for Soda', 'Lager and Ale' and 'Miss Demeanour'.

I was stunned! Breathless! Lost for words! I had found God!! Then they played 'A million Vacations' and the mighty 'Battlescar!' by a band I had vaguely heard of called Max Webster. Through the introductions on the radio, I learned that this was Kim Mitchell's previous band before he became a solo artist.

It was an epiphany. I was 'gob-smacked', as we say in Lancashire. I had to find out more about this enigma.

This "world's such a wonder".

audio fixations

Discovering 'Shaking Like a Human Being' (1986)

Saturday arrived and I had money in my pocket. Like a 23-year-old child, I boarded the train at the Victoria Park and Danforth Avenue Station. The train journey started above ground, but as it got closer to downtown Toronto the train became the sub-way. It felt like you were entering right into the belly of the city. The journey usually took around forty minutes, regardless of the day or time.

I loved downtown Toronto and I've always enjoyed city life in general. Although I was born in the English city of Manchester, from the age of six I was brought up in a rural location and I suppose it's the intense contrast in the environments that appeals to me.

I had spent many evenings and weekends exploring 'Metro' Toronto meandering its 'nooks and cranny's'. But today was different. Today I had only one destination in mind. 351 Yonge Street, Toronto. The home of A&A records and the current stockist of the album 'Shaking Like a Human Being' by Kim Mitchell.

You know how it's said that, everyone remembers where they were when Kennedy was shot? Well, I'm not trying to compare something as trivial as buying an album with the atrocity that happened in Dallas that November day, but when it comes to my musical landscape, A&A records and the purchase of 'Shaking like a Human Being' was my Kennedy moment.

I handed over my hard earned five bucks and held in my hands my definition of 'twelve inches of true love', which became my gateway album to the amazing Kim Mitchell.

On the way home, I poured over every detail of the cover and inner sleeve. It was a fairly unassuming cover really, and was full of names and credits that meant next to nothing to me at the time. The lyrics in particular, appeared to be more like weird poetry than conventional song lyrics. There didn't seem to be too much 'I love you, here's a bunch of flowers!' type of thing going on here. I must have read them a dozen times by the time I reached Crescent Town.

When I arrived home, I had the apartment to myself. Placing the record on the turntable, I turned up the volume as loud as I dared and I positioned myself equidistant between the speakers, and allowed the music to wash over me. Paul Delong's tightly tuned drums came crashing into my world, leading us into the crunching, almost 'funky' guitar and bass rhythm of the opening track 'Get Lucky (Boys and Girls)'.

The self-production was phenomenal! Robert Sinclair Wilson's simple yet solid bass, is so tightly entwined with Mitchell's guitar that you would believe in telepathy. The use of guitar layering is exquisite. The song pounds along, making you want to punch the air or pick up that air-guitar. Mitchell's vocals are incredible. Strong, powerful, deep and soulful.

And then, as a complete surprise came Peter Fredette. Words can't describe the effortless power and range in this man's voice. Without doubt one of the world's best singers. I can't work out who is the luckiest, Fredette for working with Kim Mitchell, or Mitchell for working with Pete Fredette? One thing is for sure however; their voices blend and complement each other so well, that any future Mitchell album without Fredette seemed unthinkable.

All in all, an elite ensemble of musicians. And a superb album opener!

Next up, the track that quickly became not only my favourite on the album, but also my favourite of Kim Mitchell's entire solo career (to date, that is) 'In My Shoes'.

Once again, Delong's drums start the song. But this time, as opposed to them being an introduction to the song, the drum pattern is the song. The instruments join in with Delong and swarm around the African-type drum pattern, like... African bees?

This song also introduces the subtle use of synthesisers to the album, dextrously played throughout by both Wilson and Fredette. The keyboards are never overstated, and compliment, rather than dominate proceedings; a crime committed by many in the 'synth' fixations dominated 1980s. This small act alone confirms to me how far ahead of his time Kim Mitchell has always been. And why his output, from Max to the present, never sounds dated.

Reading the credits, it became self-evident that the person responsible for the wonderful lyrics was Pye Dubois.

As I learned more, it became clear that despite not playing an instrument, Pye Dubois was very much a part of the band. A French/Canadian poet from Quebec, whose work remains criminally overlooked.

The rest of side one: 'Alana loves me', 'Patio Lanterns' and side one's closer 'That's the Hold' make up the five tracks from 'Shaking' that I had already heard, courtesy of Q107, all extremely varied, well produced, catchy and, well..., danceable. 'That's the Hold', which is similar to 'Get lucky (Boys and Girls)' in guitar sound and feel, became the band's preferred live opener, right up until the present day.

'Alana Loves Me' just blows me away. It showcases all the best elements of the entire album in just over four sweet minutes. The extremely 'sing-along' chorus is the most powerful and memorable on the disc. Once stored in the memory banks, it never leaves you. Fredette at his best.

'Patio Lanterns' was the big summer hit for Mitchell, and is tremendous. Very commercial, and maybe this was the point that the odd 'Max Webster' fan left the Mitchell camp behind them. But, if so, that was a mistake. This is pure

Mitchell/Dubois at their sublime best. As always, the production is crystal clear, and helps to lift the song to a higher place.

Make no mistake about it, though undoubtedly 'rock', this was a very commercial album. Totally deserving of its eventual, triple platinum, success.

I honestly believe that if Kim Mitchell had been a British artist, this album would have been unavoidable in the UK. It would have been a 'monster' seller there. These songs were perfect for British radio. Such a missed opportunity.

I've always had a particular and peculiar way of listening to new records. Rather than try and take it all in in one go, I tend to listen to side one a few times before moving on to side two. A trend I've continued even when compact disc came along.

After hearing side one about five times, I took a short breather, got myself a cold-one, and made myself comfortable for side two's all brand new Kim Mitchell material.

A synthesiser introduction? But nothing to worry about, just a couple of mood setting, tasteful chords to introduce the sublime, laid back beauty of 'In Your Arms'.

Lovely, light electric piano. Angelic choral effects. The lyrics describing everyone's feelings of the time they met 'the one'. Simply beautiful.

'City Girl' is a bit of bar room boogie. A fairly throwaway kind of track for this band's standards, but still immense fun nonetheless. I actually worked out and performed a version of this song during the '90s whilst fronting a band called 'Drumm'.

'Easy to Tame' immediately became a popular, crowd pleaser. Despite, or because of, the song being a little, dare I say it, simplistic...? And towards the end, a touch repetitive. Not one of my favourites, but still, a very cleverly constructed song and not to be underestimated.

The final songs of the album 'Cameo Spirit' and 'Hitting the Ground' are similar in feel to each other, and stand out as being different to the rest of the collection. Both are superbly arranged and performed.

As a newcomer to Kim Mitchell, I first found these tracks confusing. Lyrically and musically, they felt less accessible than the others. Repeated listening though, brought great reward. These were songs more reminiscent of Mitchell's past, his Max Webster days, so a little quirkier than the norm.

Once I got my head around this, I grew to love these songs as well. 'Hitting The Ground' reminds me of other album closers (that I was yet to discover) like, 'Cry Out Your Life' from 'Universal Juveniles' and 'Chain of Events' from 'Kim Mitchell'. The chorus powerfully repeating during the outro, all made perfect sense.

Wow! I was emotionally exhausted. And, as you've probably worked out by now, completely hooked. I hadn't felt like this about an artist for years. I knew for sure I was going to be a lifelong fan. But, as a record collector, I had a slight problem...

'Summer's up!' and 'turning bluc'.

homelandwonderland

Christmas was approaching and I was getting homesick. The days were getting shorter, the nights getting longer, and with it, the temperatures cooling. Each day felt more like all work and no play which was making me a dull boy! Summer was definitely over. October brought long, cold dark nights. Not that we didn't have those in England, but it felt like the honeymoon period was now over.

Rick was in Montreal, and, although I had friends in Toronto, It didn't feel the same. Also, living in Crescent Town wasn't helping matters. The 'Beaches' it was not. There was nowhere inviting to go to after work. It wasn't a bad area by any means, but I missed the evening walks along Queen Street or the boardwalk. Leisurely strolls I would have continued to undertake even through the autumn, I'm sure. Danforth Avenue was vibrant enough, but it isn't very picturesque, and the coffee houses and bars didn't look all that inviting. Am I painting a picture?

To tell the truth, after my short visit home at the end of September, I never really settled back into the way of life I had become accustomed too.

I wondered, fairly seriously, about relocating to Montreal to re-join Rick. We had recently spoken and he'd told me that there might be work at a local building company. I was sorely tempted. I'd had a great time in Montreal when I'd visited, but I knew deep down, Montreal was for me: a great place to visit, but not to live.

I'd fallen for Toronto, big style, and I knew any future for me in Canada would be in Toronto. Nowhere else.

After examining my feelings for a week or two, riding an emotional roller coaster of sadness, regret and feelings of failure? I decide it was time to return home.

Deciding to cut my stay shorter than intended meant that I needed to save as much money as possible if I wanted to get home for Christmas. This wasn't too much of a problem as there was still plenty of work, and overtime if I needed it, but needing to save money for the journey, meant I wasn't going to be able to afford to buy the back-catalogue of my new found friend Kim Mitchell. Oh! Calamity.

This was a real dilemma for me, as I knew it was unlikely the albums would be available back home. Certainly not outside of London.

I still hadn't heard much Max Webster yet, apart from the odd track on the radio, so, I had no idea which album to pick up first. I didn't even really know what was out there. As it happened, the decision was made for me.

I had borrowed a bicycle from a younger brother of a friend to help me get to and from work. I could drive, but didn't have a vehicle, so the bike came in handy. Whilst in my possession, the bike was stolen, and so I had to replace it, at a cost of around $200. Bang went my records. Oh well, worse was to follow!

I'd booked my flight back so that I would arrive in my homeland on Christmas eve. I was sad to be leaving but once the arrangements were made, I began to look forward to going home. And then... disaster.

Remember I mentioned earlier my work colleague, and friend Ted Shay? Well, unbeknownst to me, he had bought a ticket for me to see Kim Mitchell at Maple Leaf Gardens... In January!! NO!! NO!! NO!! I was absolutely distraught but I could do nothing about it. Writing this now, I realise I still haven't got over it.

Ted ended up driving me to the airport on the 23rd for my night flight home. At the airport Ted made up for my disappointment, in spades, by presenting me with a present. He'd bought me the Kim Mitchell album 'Akimbo Alogo'. I was ecstatic. I'd never even seen this album before. I am forever in Ted's debt for that one, simple gesture of kindness. The album went on to be my joint-favourite Kim Mitchell record, side by side with 'Shaking like a Human Being'.

The flight to Manchester is a long one. Seven hours. And I hate flying at night. There's nothing to see through the windows. Back then, they shut the communal TV service off partway through the flight, so people could sleep undisturbed. And I can never sleep! I therefore had plenty of time to read the cover of 'Akimbo Alogo'; credits, lyrics, the lot.

I was very pleased to see that it appeared, on the surface, to be 'business as usual' in the Mitchell camp. The same fantastic collection of musicians, with the inclusion of Tod Booth on keyboards, Pye Dubois' intriguing lyrics and, once again, Kim Mitchell in the self-production chair.

The cover itself sported a better clearer picture of Kim. You need to remember this was someone I had never seen. Three photographs were all I had to go on. An ordinary looking bloke. Understated in appearance, like on the two album covers I owned. Someone you would easily walk right past in the street, not realising that this was a God amongst men. The cover shot looked good fun though, portraying a man with a humorous side.

I didn't know it at the time but, due to the increasing anti-smoking campaigns across Europe, the cover used over here was a shot of Mitchell without the cigarette in his mouth. The same shot was also used on the compact disc covers. Political correctness gone mad once again. Art is art and should not be compromised. Surely, controversy is a good thing?

I was dying to play it. Bursting at the seams. But this time, I had a much longer wait ahead. The anticipation nearly killed me. Smoking wasn't banned on aircraft in 1986 but, after that journey, I now no longer have to wonder what smokers go through on a long-haul flight. After all, it was clear that I had an addiction too.

A couple of hours to go until we land. I was just 'two steps home'.

here among the cats

Discovering 'Akimbo Alogo' (1984)

I went home and lived with my parents at first, always the easy option. I also reacquainted myself with my record collection, with two new additions that took pride of place.

I was really itching to play the new album, but I'm not a complete anorak. I went out and got shit-faced with mates for a couple of non-stop days. Trying to tell them, and whilst slurring words and making no sense I'm sure, about this incredible, new/old artist I had discovered. Most showed no interest, but one or two seemed intrigued.

After a couple of exhausting partying days, I finally got the house to myself. The big wait was over. It was time for 'Akimbo Alogo'.

'Akimbo Alogo' is usually referred to as his first 'full length' album, as it came after his eponymous EP which I had yet to own.

The album opens with his likely most famous song from his long and illustrious career, 'Go for Soda'. Apparently, this song was even played on British radio, but not whenever I was in earshot.

The extremely catchy and memorable guitar intro, accompanied by snappy streetwise finger clicks, leads us into a rocky, driving song. It is just so uplifting, and it placed me firmly back in Toronto to the time I was working in the church, and heard this song for the first time. Everyone is on top form, once again, particularly Pye Dubois. The production seems slightly different this time around. A little less sheen than 'shaking' which gives the overall sound a rockier feel with the guitar sound dirtier and growling where needed.

The intro to 'Soda' is very deceptive in its simplicity, and is very difficult to play. The band I was in which morphed into The Universal Juveniles (more later) used to perform 'Soda' for a while. The guitarists in the band are very talented, competent, musicians, but they just couldn't work out what Mitchell was doing to get that sound and pattern. One guitarist came up with the notion that Mitchell had a "long thumb"...? The other came up with the notion that he was just a "clever bastard!" In the end, we 'riffed' the intro up and played chords instead of picking.

The rockier sound and feel are more evident on the 'rootsy', 'stripped down', second track, 'That's a Man'. Guitars all over this one. You can visualize the band cranking this one out in a small smoke and beer filled sweat pit somewhere, frightening the hell out of the locals.

Whenever I listen to this song, as a fan or a musician, I can't help but wonder where the hell he gets these arrangements from? I would not know where to begin with something like 'That's a Man'. An incredible arrangement, always interesting, as well as rocking like a swine!

I was in heaven again! If the opening tracks were any indication, this album was going to be as good, if not better, than 'Shaking'.

After the onslaught of the first two tracks, when you first hear 'All We Are', it comes as quite a shock. Deep, resonating synthesiser notes, followed by a low growling guitar, and we're into a love song. But this is Kim Mitchell and Pye Dubois. No one else writes a love song like this. The instruments create a soundscape, which successfully conjures up the image of the vast universe over which Mitchell sings of how fragile and vulnerable we are when it comes to something as powerful as love. We have absolutely no control over the situation. Easily my favourite Dubois lyric.

As if this wasn't enough, Pete Fredette forces home the image with the best vocal performance of anybody's life, not just his. An unbelievable performance which makes this song his own and places Mitchell in the supporting role in his own song.

Understandably, 'All We Are' has become a mainstay of the bands live set. Audiences, me included, wait for this song as Pete's 'moment'. Fantastic! And live, he always delivers. In my opinion, during the live version on 'Wild Party' Fredette performs better than on the studio version. An incredible voice.

Phew! Can the album maintain this standard? Oh yes it can! 'Diary for Rock 'N' Roll Men' is back to the barroom, power rock of 'That's a Man' territory. Clever arrangements, bizarre, wonderful lyrics, guitars all over the place and loud driving bass. This was definitely a rock album. Nowhere near as commercial as 'Shaking'.

Did someone mention 'commercial'?

Commerciality goes completely, out of the window with side one closer, 'Love Ties'.

If this had been the very first song that Mitchell had submitted to the record company, it's doubtful whether he would have had a career. It's not a bad song. It's a great song. But... weird! I can't imagine what a record executive would have made of this track. Luckily for us, Mitchell was so far into his successful career that he was able to create almost anything he wanted. Absolute artistic free reign. A great place to be.

'Love Ties' is a strange song though. A disjointed feel. Jerky rhythms, metallic guitar stabs. Lyrically, a little confusing. But all strangely enjoyable. Not my favourite though, and a bit of a weak finish to a very strong side one.

As before, I listened to the first side a few times before turning over. Young readers will be confused at this point. For older readers, it was time for side two.

'Feel It Burn' is a fairly straight mid-tempo rocker, similar in style to 'In Your Arms' from 'Shaking'. Superb guitar work by Mitchell, direct lyrics from Dubois. To me, this had "hit single" written all over it! Surprisingly it was never released as a single though. What a shame.

Another song Mitchell will never get away without playing in concert is the raucous party animal's call to arms 'Lager and Ale'. A song firmly in keeping with the rock theme of this album. It has a similar feel to, and belongs among 'That's a Man' and 'Diary for Rock 'n' Roll Men'. Pure rock.

'Rumour Has It' is reminiscent of 'Love Ties" quirky strangeness. It gallops along at a million miles an hour. It's almost like punk, with its speed. The baffling lyrics are mostly sung as a duet with Pete Fredette's vocals stealing the show from under Mitchell's nose.

The mood created by the last two tracks of the record is very similar to the end of 'Shaking'. Ending the album in a calmer vein than the frenetic heaviness which preceded.

'Caroline' is an unusual arrangement which is easier to follow. The lyrics, a paean to 'Caroline', are sheer poetry. Dubois excels throughout this album.

The closing track, 'Called Off', is magnificent. After everything, this seems like a very simple song but far from it. The atmosphere created by this fabulous collection of artists is simply breath-taking. The chorus is so simple, but unbearably poignant. Dubois has the ability to say so much in just a couple of lines. Powerful stuff! The beauty of this track literally brings a lump to the throat, and a tear to the eye. Although, that could be because this is the last track, leaving you heartbroken that it's over!

This time, not only had I confirmed that I had found God. But now, I'd brought him home.

The two albums were quickly recorded onto a C-90 cassette (google it) for use in the car. I ended up wearing the tape out. I played nothing else for months, which drove some people nuts. But there were a few that were impressed and the word of Kim Mitchell began to spread 'amongst the cats'!

Alas, I had no more Mitchell music. What to do? Today, I would just go onto the internet and order on-line from anywhere in the world. Back then in 1987, I had to get in the car and search record store after record store. A task I relished, if truth be told. But I had my doubts about how successful I would be. I knew that Mitchell had one other album out, the EP, but I needed to know exactly how many Max Webster albums existed.

I wasn't sure how to begin... I was in a quandary. 'Distressed'!

o' mercy leigh-anne

Once I was settled back home, I managed to get work fairly easily. There was plenty around in the building trade, although it was still poorly paid in the north of England. Much better prospects of earning good money in the capital, but I hadn't returned home to travel south. Like the saying goes, home is where the heart is.

Salaries in the building trade have much improved in Britain over the years I'm glad to say, although I left the trade behind in the '90s. Long before the pay increases arrived.

What was hardest to come by, apart from Max Webster material, was a decent band to front. The old band, Tokyo, had sadly called it a day, so I was on the prowl. I auditioned for a couple of bands and had a few rehearsals with each. Ultimately though, neither was what I was looking for.

Not long after being home, I met up with a friend of a friend, Kathy. I had known Kathy for a few months before I went to Canada. On my return, we started to spend time together. Once she heard my Kim Mitchell cassette, well... that was it. She couldn't (or wouldn't) leave me alone. We ended up renting a property together in Clitheroe.

Funnily enough, the property was owned by the mother of my good friend Rick, whom I had recently left back in Montreal. It truly is a small world.

Back on the music trail, I finally landed a great young band called Crimes of Passion, a U2 influenced type of band.

They wrote all their own material and had attracted interest on the strength of their first demo. Apparently, the record company that showed interest said that they were not too keen on the singer. The band had therefore sought a replacement and luckily found me!

We recorded a second four track demo and landed a couple of good support slots but unfortunately, the company eventually declined to take it any further.

I was beginning to get jaded by the search for a recording contract; it was becoming evident that my 'big break' wasn't going to happen. And, although only 28, I knew it was likely my opportunity had passed me by. But the 'drive and desire' was fun while it lasted.

This revelation signalled a change in musical direction for me, and against the odds, I joined the 'electro' synthesiser band I mentioned earlier, called Drumm. We performed covers of other people's material, and it was great to not have the pressure of promoting original material. I think we were pretty good and I even got them to perform a couple of Kim Mitchell songs; 'In Your Arms', which was short lived as we struggled to do it justice so it was eventually dropped from the set. Then 'City Girl' which was not my choice, but the band loved it.

'City Girl' was great fun to perform and I was in my element. The opportunity to subliminally promote Kim Mitchell to unsuspecting UK audiences gave me quite a kick!

Kathy and I were getting along very well indeed and we eventually bought a house together in the neighbouring village of Sabden, the historical home of the Pendle Witches. The surrounding area was the heartland of the medieval witch hunts and burnings in England and is situated at the foot of Pendle Hill. As an aside, Pendle Hill is only fifty feet short of being classed as a mountain under British law. It is a beautiful and picturesque part of the Ribble Valley.

We were married in September 1989, but in hindsight, our relationship was already showing signs of fragility.

Obviously, it was in dire need of an influx of new Kim Mitchell material. But eventually, even that wouldn't save it.

~~~~~~~~~~~~

October 20th 1990. Our gorgeous daughter, Leigh-Anne Elizabeth was born at 6:10am.

O Mercy! I wasn't mature enough to be a father. I wasn't mature enough to be a husband, let alone be responsible for a beautiful, dependant, little girl.

Leigh-Anne was, and is, a wonderful beautiful bundle of joy and not surprisingly, showed a very early interest in rock music. A particular fondness for Def Leppard as I recall, so things looked good.

Unfortunately, the arrival of our daughter didn't save the marriage as it surely should have. I take full responsibility for the divorce as all I wanted to do at that time, was pursue a musical path.

Kathy was a good wife and a great mother. I however, was neither ready for, nor had the strength of character required for such a commitment. I have some regrets from the period, but despite that, Leigh-Anne grew up healthy and well and, as I write this, is attending University. She has never been out of my life and we've been there for each other every day.

Kathy went on to find true happiness and security so hopefully, all ended well there.

~~~~~~~~~~~~

Outside of my relationship challenges, where was Kim Mitchell? It was time to, 'fill my head with rock'!

research (at record stores)

Discovering 'Kim Mitchell' (1982)

In Clitheroe, there was a small record store at which I was a frequent patron. Through the shops reference books, and research at the local library, I managed to collate the titles of all the Max Webster albums that existed. None of which, unfortunately, were available to me as they were all on import. I needed to visit the cities; Manchester, Birmingham, London etc. The search was on!

The first port of call was Manchester. My birthplace and the nearest city centre to me; about an hour's drive away.

I struck gold at Virgin mega store, Market Street, the first store I visited. Unbelievable! There in the rack, being ignored by all and sundry, with letters which appeared ten feet tall to me, was Kim's debut solo recording, the 'Kim Mitchell' EP. It was crying out to me in the loudest voice.

The album had a big import sticker on it, which was really just an excuse for the exorbitant price tag attached. £12. That's $24 to you Canadians. For five tracks? Absolutely. I didn't flinch and handed the money over for the find of the century.

I hoped I might be on a roll that day, and stumble upon most, if not all, the Max albums. I visited all the record emporiums I knew, including a few second-hand stores, but my first find was to be my last that day. However, I was overjoyed at my one purchase and I hot-footed it back home to crank up the volume.

The cover of 'Kim Mitchell' was simplistic but is by far the most striking of the three covers I had to date. On this one, Kim looks as though he really means business. And he most definitely does!

Personnel wise, all the boys were 'present and correct'. With shaking hands, I placed the needle in the groove, and prepared myself to be blown away.

'Kids In Action' has a southern, swampy feel to it. Lynyrd Skynyrd would be proud of this one. We are in the barroom band territory of 'Lager and Ale' and 'That's a Man' land here. A rollicking opener which effectively lays out Mitchell's solo intent from the off.

The conspicuous lack of keyboards here, and throughout the record, is perhaps a deliberate act of intent to let go of the past, as keyboards were such an integral part of the overall Max Webster sound.

'Miss Demeanour' is magnificent, and quite possibly, the highlight of this short collection. A fun, light rhythm with clever wordplay from Dubois, sweet bass runs from Wilson alongside the first indications of Fredette's vocals (here joined by Bernie LaBarge), and capped off with some pleasing Spanish style acoustic guitar work. An outstanding track. Strangely, not one he has returned to in a live context though.

'Big Best Summer' continues in the heavy vein, and is a song that, in the future, I will find reminiscent of Max's 'Hangover'. Driven along by DeLong's rock steady drums and flashy fills and with Mitchells off-kilter, descending chord patterns. It's hard to believe that this is basically, a three-piece band in action. There's always something new cropping up with repeated listening.

'Tennessee Water' enforces the southern feel of 'Kids in Action'. It's an up-tempo swinger with a country tinge. You could easily line dance to this one, and I've had to stop myself doing just that on a number of occasions. Superbly played and great fun. The band sounds as though they really enjoyed themselves on this record.

'Chain Of Events'. The final track? It's too short! why? Oh well… An awesome closer. Incredibly atmospheric. It has a similar feel to 'Mutiny Up My Sleeve' era Max. A typically complicated arrangement which just sucks the listener in. DeLong's drumming is sensational. The outro is classic Mitchell. A repeated pattern to the fade which, even though it's probably long enough, you just don't want it to end. In fact, if he'd carried on playing it for another twenty minutes, it would have been a complete album, time wise. Well... I'd have been happy, anyway!

That was it. Another true masterpiece. The three albums would keep me going for a while, but I had it bad. I needed more, and fast.

After all, it was my 'Rock 'n' Roll duty'!

wander, where and why

Discovering 'Universal Juveniles' (1980)

In another example of life before the internet being unkind to fans knowing about album releases across the pond, in 1989, Kim Mitchell had released a new album called 'Rockland', and just over 12 months later, also unleashed 'I Am a Wild Party (Live)'.

I was clearly oblivious to this as I set off to wander around the North and Midlands of England, 'in search of Max Webster'. I was happy to journey as far south as Birmingham, but for now, London would have to wait.

I travelled many miles, even covering Wales, but I had no joy. Despondent, I began to make my way home. And then... I called into a second-hand record store in Blackburn; a town only ten miles from me. I had zero expectations on entering the dusty establishment, so imagine my utter amazement when I came across, not one, but two Max Webster albums! 'A Million Vacations' and 'Universal Juveniles'!

They were both a bit sorry looking, with torn covers, but I still couldn't help salivating over them. Who in their right mind had decided to part with these treasures? Which fool had needed, so desperately, a few pence rather than hang on to these two wonders?

For me, they were gold dust, and would cost me only £1.50 each. 'Lost lovers found' or what?

I was aware that 'Universal Juveniles' had been Max's last album, so deciding to continue my trend of playing artists albums in reverse order, I played 'Universal Juveniles' first.

Wow! What a cover! I could imagine how some of my friends might have balked at the image of this thin white dude dressed in yellow lycra but, come on! This was Kim Mitchell and Max Webster. Ground breaking and iconic!

This time, there was a neat, inner sleeve, with the lyrics, accompanied by weird, and wonderful, drawings, created by Greg Elliott. This already looked as though it was going to be a strange trip.

So, here goes! My first hearing, ever, of an entire Max Webster album. Ok, so I was a late starter. Fifteen years too late actually, but we always remember the first time.

For 'Universal Juveniles', the Max Webster line up was: Kim Mitchell, Gary McCracken, drums, and Dave Myles, bass, with Dave Stone guesting on keyboards. Terry Watkinson, an integral part of Max's history, had left the band by this time, but did make a dramatic appearance on the album, as I'll explain in due course.

All this meant little to me at the time. I knew nothing of Max Webster's history. With these musicians' names being new to me, my only concern was whether they could even come close to matching the talent on display in the Kim Mitchell band. There was only one way to find out.

Opening track, 'In the World of Giants', pre-dates speed metal by, at least, ten years. But... here it is. Proof, once again, of how far ahead of the pack Mitchell has always been. The song stampedes from the speakers, and lays waste to all who dare to stand in its way. An intricate arrangement again. The band firing on all cylinders and incredibly tight. Superbly produced by Jack Richardson. It leaves your senses numbed and your mind confused about what it has just experienced.

Not an easy first introduction, by any means, and, after the first hearing, I was left a bit unsure. Don't worry though, like all good things that need time to mature, repeated listening pays off. This is a fantastic opener, to a fantastic album. The rest of the album is easier to digest right off the bat.

'Check' is a storming, AC/DC type of rocker, but much better. It's a stop-start kind of introduction song. A sound check, getting all the levels right, blast! "Here we are, loud and proud". No one will resist. I believe this would have been a good contender as the album opener.

There's no let up from the onslaught with track three, 'April in Toledo'. McCracken and Miles working together here, as everywhere on the album, to create their own wall of sound. McCracken's drumming style appears heavier than DeLong's, making Max, possibly, more rock than Mitchell's solo output. Although the production contributes to that perception also.

Kim's vocals on the album are dependably magnificent and his delivery of Pye's tongue-twisting couplets is unbelievable. My current band, The Universal Juveniles, recorded three tracks from this record (more of this later), and they were the hardest songs I've ever had to perform in over thirty years. When you hear this album again, don't underestimate Mitchell's phrasing and diction, lesser mortals couldn't achieve what Mitchell accomplishes here. Phenomenal!

'Juveniles Don't Stop' drops the tempo, ever so slightly, but not the intensity. A steadier drum beat throughout gives the impression of a respite, but the theme of the song, the power and ambition of youth, is right in keeping with everything that's gone before. The guitars have a less metal feel here, touching almost, on Mitchell's occasional forays into a southern sounding groove.

Side one closes with the epic 'Battlescar'. The song I held in my hands all those years ago in that little record shop in Blackburn, Lancashire. If I had taken that record home with me back in 1980, the path of my life would have taken such a different route. I would have become a fan straight away. Maybe even got to see Max live? Just the thought makes me cry…

'Battlescar' is, of course, the duet with Rush, and also sees the welcome return of Terry Watkinson.

Without even hearing the track, you know it's going to be special. How can it not be? Gary McCracken and Neil Peart? Alex Lifeson and Kim Mitchell? Geddy Lee and Dave Myles? Not to mention Lee and Mitchell's joint vocal attack.

The song is written by Mitchell and Dubois, and so is definitely the property of Max Webster, Rush guest on the track, at their own request.

An unusual start, with two consecutive bass solos, which announce the arrival of McCracken and Peart's loud and stomping, tribal drum beats. Then Mitchell's deep, rich vocals resonate before Lee and then the rest of the ensemble join in with full force.

A slow, atmospheric number which is simmering with foreboding – Neil Peart was later to call it 'Wagnerian' in delivery? The choral crescendo, which repeats longer than one might expect, is a genius touch.

The performance of both bands is electrifying. An incredible side one closing. And a hard act to follow!

Side two opens with 'Chalkers'. The frantic pace of the album discernibly slowing now. More texture and light and shade, with Stone's sweet keyboard flourishes prominent for the first time on the album. Driven along by a bubbling bass and guitar, there's plenty of room for Mitchell to breathe on this one. A welcome breather, after the frenzied power of side one.

'Drive And Desire' picks up the pace a little with a guitar driven boogie reminiscent of 'Big Best Summer' from Mitchell's EP. McCracken's drum fills here are fast, furious and excellent. A great track!

Next up is, for me, the centrepiece of the album; 'Blue River Liquor Shine'.

A powerful staccato, bass and piano intro alongside 'Battlescar' type drum beats, leading into a folk/country style acoustic verse, with tasteful tambourine accompaniment. The dynamics between the heavy chorus and stripped, acoustic verses are superb. Dave Stone's delicate piano in the chorus and outro are an invaluable added touch. Another fade-out which for me, could have carried on longer. If anyone agrees, check out the Universal Juveniles version.

'What Do You Do with The Urge' begins in a similar fashion to 'Drive and Desire' but, part way through, changes to an, almost jazz type chill out.

Repeated listening to this album reveals, so many, different styles and variations. A master class in progressive musicianship. Simply breath taking!

'Cry out Your Life' ends the album in dramatic form. The song, in most part, all on the same chord. An extremely potent and doom laden, Sabbath-style composition which, just at the very end switches and lifts the song to a lighter more uplifting fade out, with a surprise false ending. Formidable!

A very powerful, fast, frenetic, furious and loud album for sure. But, hidden in the grooves, you'll find a lot of texture, colour and finesse. An incredible album. Perhaps one that you need to invest a bit of time in to fully appreciate.

For a band album, this is clearly Mitchell's moment and could have, quite easily, been his first solo record. A record which I consider to be one of, if not the best Max Webster albums.

This was the bands last album and definitely a high point musically in their career. But why did they call it a day? Surely this was a great album to continue an even greater career?

For Mitchell however, if not for anyone else, it had obviously been the time to 'let go the line'.

a party

Discovering 'A Million Vacations' (1979)

'A Million Vacations' was arguably Max Webster's most successful album, sonically and critically. It was the bands only platinum selling album so it was clearly their best commercial success. With this success, they finally started to make a few waves in Europe.

In Britain there was the Top of the Pops appearance with 'Paradise Skies', a support slot throughout Europe with stable mates Rush and even two headlining shows at the famous Marquee Club in London. Annoyingly, as I've mentioned before, all missed by yours truly!

As 'Universal Juveniles' was Max's rock album, 'Vacations', is without doubt, their most commercial album. From the title to the cover, with its postcards and beach balls, this is a fun time party album all the way. Potential hit singles abound. The magnificent production, by John de Nottbeck and the band themselves, is lavish, bright and sunny.

The opening track, 'Paradise Skies' lets you know the bands intent from the off. "Paradise is beginning to ride!" Dave Myles' bass is well to the fore on this, and elsewhere, helping to give an almost pop feel right across the album.

The separation of the instruments in production gives a very clean sound and is at times a little too 'sterile' in places in my opinion. But I'm nit-picking. I wouldn't want all their albums to sound the same after all! It's a real fun opener.

'Charmonium', written by Terry Watkinson, has a hip summer of love feel to it and swings along wonderfully. There are more keyboards on this album than on other albums, which is no bad thing. The interplay between keys and guitar is exceptional. Proggy in places, pop in others, and only displays the diversity and compositional skills of this great band.

Mitchell perhaps relinquished the reins slightly on this album, allowing four of the ten tracks to be presented by other members of the band. Three from Watkinson and one from McCracken. Apart from the lead vocal delivery on some tracks, you can't spot the join. 'Charmonium' and the others, fit in with the overall Max sound seamlessly.

Third track; 'Night Flights', a rare Watkinson/Dubois writing collaboration sung by Mitchell, is simply storming. Similar in feel to 'Paradise Skies'. 'Myles' bass work, played in tandem with Watkinson's synth bass, seems to be the driving force of most of these songs. McCracken is as tight and as powerful as ever.

The last two tracks of side one segues together, and have the feel of being part of the same structure. 'Sun Voices' is the albums ballad and is smothered in glorious texture and beauty. Although a Mitchell/Dubois song, Watkinson's keyboards are again, heavily involved in the mix along with a luscious string arrangement. Mitchell's vocal performance is exemplary here. Singing at the top of his range, he delivers with a superb pained fragility. A mournful feeling pervades the song, leaving you feeling incredibly maudlin. Strong stuff indeed.

The instrumental masterpiece 'Moon Voices' ends side one on a psychedelic note. An opportunity for the restrained virtuosos to finally shine. The piece, the last part in Pye Dubois' 'Moon' Quadrilogy, is a blast! Gary McCracken excels here. His sharp, snappy drum rolls the centrepiece of a great swooping kaleidoscopic soundscape.

Side two begins with the album's title track. 'A Million Vacations', written by McCracken/Dubois and sung by Gary.

This band were really in a party mood when they entered Phase One studios to record this album.

A Glam Rock classic which, even now, is possibly Max's most played summer song on Canadian radio. Hats off to Pye Dubois and Gary McCracken. The song is fantastic! So much fun. It reminds me of the best moments of 70's radio when T-Rex or Sweet were always being played. A great song for the car or anywhere, for that matter. And McCracken makes a cracking (sorry!) job of the vocals. Brilliant!

'Look Out' is another bright, upbeat number with a killer chorus. Equal parts guitar and keys with Myles' bass notes bubbling underneath like 'Chalker' from 'Juveniles'.

The instrumental break near the end of the song, is unusual, even for Max Webster's standards. A light jazz affair, delicately constructed, with the dreamy end section similar in style to the mighty 'Gravity' from 'High Class in Borrowed Shoes'. Mind blowing!

Next up is Watkinson's solo-penned superb 'Let Go the Line'. Strangely, my favourite on the record. I don't know why I like this song so much, but it sounds to me like a very '70s middle of the road kind of song. In lesser hands, it would have been mediocre at best. Here, Max created a thing of true beauty. Understated and fragile. It should have become a club standard throughout the North American continent and made Watkinson a rich man. Sometimes, there is no justice in the world.

'Rascal Houdi'. Back in classic familiar Max territory here. Reassuringly weird and wonderful. See 'Toronto Tontos' and 'Let Your Man Fly' as reference points. Terrific interplay. Great fun!

Last up is the jam along 'Research (At Beach Resorts)'. Obviously tightly rehearsed but made to sound spontaneous and fresh. Not necessarily in keeping with the rest of the album, with its live crowd noises and loose feel. It is, nevertheless, outstanding. Not sure whether it is live or just designed to sound live? Thematically, it's right in step with the rest of 'Vacations', and ends the album much as it began, on a high!

From the production, through the performances to the album sleeve art, this was always going to be the commercial success it was. For Max Webster, it is different. But it definitely works. Joyous!

Wow! A double delight for me. Two at once. I now had plenty to keep me going. But there were four more albums to find. London was calling. It was time to saddle-up!

Would London astonish me? It would, but in a frustratingly negative way.

getting back what's gone

Things away from the Kim Mitchell and Max Webster obsession were going pretty well. I had landed a new job which paid well and was very laid back. I was enjoying a completely, stress free existence.

The band, Drumm, had dispensed with the '80s electro path and had augmented the line up with the recruitment of a couple of fine musicians. We had more work than we knew what to do with, even turning venues away as we couldn't fit them into our schedule. A very nice position to be in, let me tell you.

The high demand for our musical services helped our agents in negotiating, and getting, a higher price tag for us. The money was tremendous, the bank account looked healthy, and life was good. The only downside to the change in the bands fortune was that we now had to perform material which the audience were guaranteed to be familiar with. We were, essentially, a dance band. I didn't have a problem with that, at all. But it meant I couldn't persuade them to perform any Max or Mitchell songs. Not even 'Let Go the Line'. We had even said goodbye to 'City Girl'. A sad day. A very sad day!

Out of the blue, I received a letter from a friend of mine in Sudbury, Ontario. This was the age before mobile phone texting and e-mails remember. She was just filling me in on things in general, and asking how I was. I hadn't thought about Canada for quite some time. What, with marriage, divorce, a daughter, the band, I'd had a lot on my plate. But the letter brought back a lot of emotions and memories and I began to think about returning. At that particular time though, it wasn't impossible but it seemed impractical. I had just landed a great new job, and the band was doing tremendously, so I put the thought on the back burner.

Towards the end of the letter, she asked me if it would be possible for me to send her some car 'air-fresheners'? Now, I know what you're thinking. I must know some really exciting fun people to be around. The kind who knows where all the good parties are; "air-fresheners" indeed!

She had visited England in the past, and one of her memories was of these quite common air fresheners for cars designed to mimic our British traffic lights. They were tall (but small) and had the three colours of red amber and green and she wanted me to send her a couple of dozen. I was more than willing to oblige, but the request got me thinking. In return, could I ask she locate for me and send over four Max Webster albums? (Their debut 'Max Webster', 'High Class in Borrowed Shoes', 'Mutiny Up My Sleeve' and 'Live Magnetic Air').

A few days later, I sent her a parcel of car fresheners, complete with my request and began to wait with bated breath!

In the meantime, hearing from Canada had really set something in motion within me, and I applied to Canada House for an immigration form. Even for me, the act seemed sudden, and honestly, didn't have much planning at all. I awoke one morning, and just sent for the form. Even I was surprised.

So, I had a couple of things to wait for, and the suspense was killing me. I had a bit of time off from the band, so I contacted some friends living in Weybridge, Surrey, which is just a short train ride from London. I packed a small bag, and went visiting and record hunting in the record album capital of Europe.

London is still probably the best place I know to go record hunting. Even though today, as with everywhere, store after store has closed down, back in early 1990, in one small area of Leicester Square and Piccadilly Circus, there were three huge major record stores. Virgin, Tower Records, and HMV. All superbly stacked to the rafters with goodies. What's more, there were plenty of smaller emporiums all within easy reach and well worth a look. All sadly gone now but back then, this was my kind of heaven. A paradise!

Although I hoped the Max albums were on their way to me from Canada, once here in the capital, I was not about to pass up the chance of buying the albums if I came across them. Money in my wallet, I was once more, 'in search of Kim Mitchell'.

After four hours searching, I was devastated. I had found absolutely nothing. It was worse than that though. What I had found was empty Max Webster racks! All the albums named, but empty! Sold out! Gone! The lousy bastards. Hadn't they known I was coming? What had they got the albums in for in the first place, if it wasn't for the sole purpose of selling them to me? And why leave the empty and titled spaces there? Was it just to torment me?

A five hundred mile, wasted round trip. I was pissed off! I could have telephoned the stores ahead of time, I know. But collectors enjoy the hunt. There is no better feeling than rifling through that garage sale or flea market and stumbling on that long lost missing piece of treasure. The 'Holy Grail'. The hunt is a major part of it all. Disappointments included. But, the agony in London didn't stop there. In Tower Records, just for my, perverse delectation, was another empty rack for... wait for it... 'Rockland' by Kim Mitchell. What? What was this? What was going on?

Have you ever seen a grown man cry? Not a pretty sight. I was gutted. One of the worst days of my record-collecting life! Not only was I going to return home empty handed without the four discs I had hoped to buy, I was now going home with five records short. Four kicks in the teeth, with a quick fifth for good measure. Bloody London! You can keep it! Give me the north, anytime. They know how to treat their record collectors. Of course, it could have all been sour grapes.

Perhaps, when I got home, there would be something in the post which would help in 'blowing the blues away'?

ear service

Discovering 'Max Webster' (1975)

Well... There were no records from Canada waiting for me upon my return. I suppose it was early days really. What there was though, was my immigration application forms from Canada House. I was incredibly nervous as I read through the surprisingly short form.

It appeared, whilst reading through the, "qualifying points" system, that I would pass with flying colours. I spoke English, but not French. I was a qualified carpenter, and my 'age grouping' was bang on the money. I filled out the form, without thinking too long or hard about it, posted it, and put it out of my mind.

A few weeks later, I received notification that a 'large' parcel was waiting for me at the post office collections depot. I ran all the way. Sure enough, the parcel was slim, approximately 12" x 12", and had a Canadian postage mark on it. I whooped with joy; Leaping and punching into the air. I couldn't bring myself to open it there and then though, in case I got mugged and somebody ran off with my new found booty! On the way home I even tried to work out whether the parcel was thick enough for four albums? Or was there only the one record inside? I was tormenting myself. I needed to get home. Fast!

Once home, I placed the parcel on a chair, and prepared myself a drink, glancing at my prize every two seconds. I was delaying opening it. The disappointment of the London visit was still too fresh in my memory. I couldn't face another setback like that.

A sudden, horrible thought came crashing into me. What if someone was playing a cruel trick on me, and inside this box was a... Donny Osmond record! Or something just as horrifying?

Oh! Grow up! I opened up the parcel.

The glorious bounty was revealed to me. All four albums. I was in heaven. I laid the covers out on the floor and just gazed upon their glory. Strange covers. For instance, I didn't understand Terry Watkinson's cover painting of the 'booze-heads' on the debut album. We don't have beer stores like they have in Ontario, you see. But it looked intriguing. The cover of 'Mutiny Up My Sleeve' seemed strangely dark and minimalist. The childlike cartoon representation of the band, in concert on Live Magnetic Air. And then... the majesty of one of my favourite covers of all time; 'High Class in Borrowed Shoes'.

Here for the first time, was a clear large portrait of what was fast becoming my favourite band of all time. And what a portrait! They looked as though they were from another planet. Planet Max! They looked fantastic! The band's pose on this cover was so memorable, that the current band I was in would try to replicate it for part of our album cover. Only the positions, mind you, not the clothing... we're not that crazy.

I broke my trend of playing the albums in reverse order here and decided to go straight to the beginning. It was time for the debut; 'Max Webster'.

Two new additions to the line-up for me this time: Paul Kersey on drums and Mike Tilka on bass. Interesting! There was a familiar name in the producer's chair, Terry Brown. 'Broon' as he was affectionately known by Rush when he produced eight of their first nine studio albums (their debut was self-produced) and their first two live albums. A formidable producer. A great ear for the dramatic. Things were looking good.

The album opens with guitar feedback over which Paul Kearsey introduces himself with a solid, well produced and meaty drum rhythm. Mitchell's feedback then becomes a heavy descending chord riff of immense power, and we're off!

'Hangover'! This was Max's first recorded offering and, once heard, things would never be the same again. Instantly memorable. The band cook up a storm. The production is top notch. A touch rougher around the edges than 'Vacations'. More of a live feel which is just the way I like it. Mike Tilka sounds great playing a million bass notes to drive the song along. Mitchell's voice is strong and mature, sounding like a seasoned pro already. Nothing on this opening track, or ensuing album, sounds like a band in its infancy. They obviously set the bar at a ridiculously high standard right off the bat. Other Toronto bands must have quivered in their boots when they first heard Max Webster!

'Here Among the Cats' is a bluesy, jazz inflected number with a '60s feel, both lyrically and with Watkinson's swirling Hammond organ sounds. Trippy, with a great feel.

Next up is Terry Watkinson's understated 'Blowing the Blues Away'. A country song, but with unusual time signatures. For a debut album, this band were not interested in playing it safe. Fantastically arranged and performed, the song sounds very simple but is far from it. Sadly, I believe Watkinson doesn't look back on this song with too much fondness, thinking it naïve. I'm here to tell you, he's wrong. This is a wonderful track. So there!

How many variations in style are on this storming debut? 'Summer Turning Blue' is a spacey, dreamy, piano led ballad. Beautiful acoustic guitar and angelic, choral backing vocals making the whole experience extremely atmospheric. Dubois' lyrics here are heart rending. Superb

Side one closes with the bizarre, off-kilter 'Toronto Tontos'. Just simply, downright weird. But... fabulous! The band displaying how tight and experimental an outfit they are. A muso's dream.

The other side begins with Dubois' first instalment in his 'moon' saga. The classic 'Coming Off the Moon'. A fairly straight, heavy rock/metal song. The guitars bright and loud. Kearsey's drums are the driving force here, with a superbly played, busy rhythm. A tight stop/start, instrumental section with fast drum rolls, a nod to other 'erstwhile' metal bands out there on how it should be done. Wonderful stuff!

Fast and furious, the uplifting joyous fun of 'Only Your Nose Knows' smacks you right on the... well, nose! A simple lyrical theme, but the lines twisted expertly by Dubois and delivered with great humour by Mitchell. This, amongst many others, must have been a bar room favourite in their early days. A real storm.

'Summers Up' is a hidden gem. Easy to overlook on first listening, but if you delve deeper into the song, this contains everything that places Max Webster head and shoulders above the rest of the pack. Deftly performed, it hints at where Max, musically, would be heading in the not too distant future.

Watkinson, who isn't as prominent on this album as he would later be, provides service to this song beautifully. His light, other-worldly touches making this song a sheer cosmic delight. Tilka's bass work, along with Mitchells acoustic guitar is sublime. A jazzy feel which leads, expertly, into the album closer.

'Lily', unlike the rest of the record, is an out and out 'prog' song. There are touches of 'prog' all over Max's work, but here they don't try to hide it. Emerson, Lake and Palmer, or King Crimson would have been proud of this one. No discernible chorus or pattern, it meanders, gorgeously, across its own landscape. Once you're delivered at its dramatic conclusion, the whole journey appears much shorter than its impressive 7.42 minutes.

A brave and emotional end to an eclectic debut.

For a bands debut record, simply unbelievable! Diverse, Imaginative and experimental. Performed with such panache as if to appear as though they had been around for years. A master class in record making.

I was absolutely floored! As you can probably tell, I could not get over the fact that this was a debut record. Most bands would have settled for this set as the pinnacle of their career.

As for myself, I still had three more new albums to play. It looked as though the bad times of the London memory were, well and truly, behind me.

oh wow!

Discovering 'High Class in Borrowed Shoes' (1977)

'High Class in Borrowed Shoes'!
This simply put is one of, if not the, greatest rock albums of all time. As a review, I shouldn't have to write any more than the title. Enlightened critics and fans alike would just sigh and nod to each other, approvingly and knowingly.

The start of the definitive Max Webster line up, with the introduction of the mighty Gary McCracken on drums.

Produced again by Terry Brown, the album opens with the machine gun barrage of the title track. Mitchell's guitar chops, sounding, at times, reminiscent of Bernard Herman's theme from 'Psycho'. Unnerving! The production is exemplary. Watkinson finally coming to the fore with his imaginative synthesiser work cutting through magnificently. The balance between the instruments is right on the money. A formidable opener.

For me, the next two tracks are the highlights of the album, although I have to reiterate that the whole album is of an incredibly high standard and to me, faultless.

Sonically surprising, track two slows the album down to a snail's pace, with the sheer majesty of 'Diamonds Diamonds'. Sounding like a Dubois poem set to incidental music. It is simply magnificent! This time the band create ambient soundscapes, twenty years before it was invented.

Watkinson takes the lead here; his light keyboard touches swimming in deep oceans of colours. The song is awash with angelic backing vocals. Then, one by one the rest of the musicians delicately introduce themselves. Dexterous and intelligent. A clear example of 'less is more'.

Is there no end to the surprises that this band continues to present? The answer is an emphatic, no!

Oh, joy of joys! 'Gravity'! My all time, absolute, desert island disc, classic, favourite, number one Max song. It's creations such as 'Gravity' that either make other musicians hang up their boots in a resigned manner, or strive to raise their own standards. Hopefully, there's more of the latter. For those who give up, I fully understand and sympathise.

A mini opera, there is so much going on here that it's hard to keep track. The unusual delivery style, by Mitchell, of Pye's superb lyrics, successfully portraying a troubled man's thoughts. We are actually inside the narrator's head, as he sits on a cloud and contemplates where his life may be heading. Such an incredibly emotive piece of music. Terry Brown's production is second to none.

I wanted so much to record a version of 'Gravity' for our own album, but we didn't even know where to begin to achieve a satisfactory version. In the end, determined to not leave the track out totally, we recorded our own 'tossed coin' sound effect, similar to the one in 'Gravity', and placed it within another song. More of a nod and a wink to Max's superiority.

The album moves into a folk phase with the next track, the heart rending 'Words to Words'. An acoustic love song. Beautifully performed. Mournful vocals. Deftness and delicacy of touch from all. Outstanding!

Despite the war zone attack of the opening track, you may be forgiven in thinking that this was going to be Max's softer, ballad filled album. Side two closer, 'America's Veins', blows that theory out of the water.

A storming and powerfully loud rock song. Everyone, almost up to eleven! Chunky metal guitar. McCracken is in full force and flow. Direct and to the point, it assaults the senses and takes no prisoners. The inspired, faltering ending matching the listeners' confused emotions after such a diverse set of songs.

Wow! I felt emotionally drained and needed to get some air before listening to side two. After a short stroll I felt as though I had collected my scattered senses back from the four winds, and was ready for more.

A low, almost subliminal hum, and then an unexpected staccato, machine gun fire burst of intense, shocking power and 'Oh War!' is unleashed upon us. Kim Mitchell's deliberately distorted, angry vocals spitting 'venomously' over this late '60s sounding, 'heavy rock' behemoth.

Heavy, heavy stuff!

Another shock to the senses! 'On The Road' returns us to the acoustic, folk song feel of 'Words to Words' territory. For Mitchell and Dubois, a very simple song, both lyrically and musically, and a welcome respite after the intensity of 'Oh War!'. Magnificently presented but due to its simplicity, probably gets overlooked on an album which contains so many heavyweights. A lovely 'feel good' song though.

Terry Watkinson's 'Rain Child', a gorgeous homage to the 'summer of love', truly begins to display what a formidable song writer he was becoming. Great guitar work from Mitchell, contrasting effectively with the druggy feel of Watkinson's keys and Tilka's understated and solid bass work, all held together by McCracken's strong and steady, dependable rhythm. Terrific!

In Context of the Moon' closes the record in prog-tastic fashion. Dubois' masterpiece. In places, the song swings... No shit! Sinatra could have had fun with this one. The song is heavy though, probably too heavy for ol' blue eyes. It shifts and slides from style to style. Sublime interplay between the musicians, intricate, full on instrumental sections, spacious verse sections, wailing guitars, tricky, fast, keyboard runs. A wonderful mix of styles and tempos. Whenever I hear it, it always makes me wonder what a brass section would sound like, if it were thrown into the mix.

Just a phenomenal, diverse, intricate and emotional, thought-provoking group of musicians. Awe-inspiring! I was shell-shocked. Kim Mitchell and Max Webster, inclusive of Pye Dubois, were beginning to affect my life in ways that I couldn't conceive of.

I wasn't aware at the time, but a 'chain of events' had begun to be set into motion.

pandemonium

Discovering 'Mutiny Up My Sleeve' (1978)

Once more produced by Terry Brown, sonically this album feels different to the other Max albums. Not 'bad' different, but it does have a different vibe somehow. Less layered and stripped back.

In a surprising twist, Mike Tilka is credited with mixing and production duties here, alongside Terry Brown, but relinquishes his role in the band as bass player to newcomer Dave Myles. Maybe that's the new vibe?

The album opens with the straight blues rock of 'Lip Service'. Guitar driven, with a good live feel. Mitchell's guitar, single tracked and sounding quite metallic. Only Watkinson's prominent Hammond organ stopping the song from being full on, mid-tempo, heavy metal boogie. A good song, but for me, an underwhelming opener. However, Dubois' lyrics and Mitchell's delivery lift the song way above the average.

A real shift in style and mood for the next track, Terry Watkinson's astounding 'Astonish Me'. One of my favourite tracks from the album. The sublime piano and synthesiser opening is just so moving. As the rest of the band join Watkinson, it almost sounds like a fanfare introduction. Stirring stuff!

Sung by Mitchell, this is one of Watkinson's best lyrics, but Mitchell puts so much of himself into this, it's hard to believe he didn't have any input. The song swoops and glides beautifully, with Watkinson's keyboards a highlight throughout. During the songs mood swings you also begin to get a sense of what an asset Dave Myles is to proceedings, a wonderful bass player, with great feel and emotion.

Next up is the second contribution by Watkinson with the surprising 'Let Your Man Fly'. Surprising as this is a guitar song. Along the same lines as 'Lip Service'; a metal song, with a bluesy, R'n'B groove. Both this and 'Lips' sound as though they may have been recorded 'live' in the studio. Better than 'Lips', it's light and fun. Mitchell's solo is excellent, and he also appears to have a great time with Watkinson's lyrics.

'Water Me Down' slows things down and returns us to the dreamy landscapes visited on 'Astonish me'. Similar in style to 'Diamonds Diamonds' and 'Words to Words'. A beautiful Dubois poem. Delicate and mournful. A pure love song. Superbly performed, it simply melts the heart.

'Distressed' closes side one in tremendous fashion. A fusion of prog, metal and jazz; an incredible arrangement. Watkinson's piano chords, underneath Mitchell's distorted guitar, is a genius touch. McCracken's contribution here is magnificent; cow bells, tambourines, kitchen sink... the phrase 'the devil is in the detail' always applies to Max Webster, and nowhere more so than here. There are even wonderful female vocals provided by Carla Jenson and Judy Donnelly. An outstanding track.

Side two opens with 'The Party'.

When myself and Mick, the drummer from our current band, The Universal Juveniles, first met Gary McCracken, he discovered that we were a Max tribute act and asked Mick...

"Can you play The Party?"
Before Mick had a chance to reply, Gary continued:
"No. No one can!"

He was right, of course. We couldn't.

A Maxterpiece, from start to finish. Another one of those arrangements that boggles the mind. Who starts these things? The ideas for these songs obviously originate from a different planet than the one we mere mortals inhabit. Incredible stuff!

A live crowd, chanting and counting the band in, then... pandemonium! A totally incomprehensible wig out! Just as difficult to describe as (I'm sure) it was to write and perform. The band at their very best, in all aspects. Prog, jazz, narrative, heavy metal, comedy. Another mini opera. Wonderful.

Oh, And Gary McCracken is unbelievable here!

Maybe, somewhere in the world, there is a drummer that can perform this song as good as McCracken? I strongly doubt it!

Things calm down considerably with the easy accessibility of 'Waterline'. A laid back, southern rock boogie. Swampy and groove laden, with its 4/4 simplicity. A good song, but nothing outstanding. A nice breather though, after 'The Party'.

The album rises to astronomical heights with the last two numbers. First up, the acoustic guitar and piano instrumental 'Hawaii'. The sound of surf and seagulls mingles with the up-tempo, jig of life instruments which interplay cleverly with each other. With superb vocal harmony accompaniment from both the band and Carla and Judy, once more. The song leaves you on an incredible high. An overlooked classic.

As with 'Gravity', from 'High Class in Borrowed Shoes', I wanted to pay homage to Hawaii on our tribute album. So, we secreted the sound of seagulls, surf and a yawn into a different song. We're pretty pleased with the results.

'Mutiny Up My Sleeve' closes with its centrepiece, 'Beyond the Moon'. Pye's moon saga, part three. Other worldly, a symphonic gem. Mitchell works overtime here, his lightning-fast guitar licks are blisteringly excellent and powerful. Very emotive.

Introduced with a quick burst of Greek/Russian style guitar and boot stomping Cossacks, the song kicks in and blows up the speakers. Extremely dramatic, with Watkinson's heavy, prominent, Hammond, eventually, giving way to tasteful, light, electric piano. An incredible mix of moods and melodies which take wing into the stratosphere.

Mitchell intones with great feel and emotion some of Dubois greatest lyrical achievements.

The finale of this song is sonic proof of Kim Mitchell's place as one of the finest guitar players to ever pick up the instrument. An extended outro solo with exasperating arpeggios over an amazing chord sequence will leave you breathless. This is the best ending to any of Mitchell's albums and is so powerful and memorable to fans that Kim has segued into this finale on a number of occasions in his solo performances.

Mind-blowing! In my top three Max songs of all time.

Wow! Again. From inauspicious beginnings, this album ends up leaving you emotionally drained and exhausted. A rollercoaster ride of many styles and emotions.

I was unable to take any more just at the moment. I was numb! My senses were completely shot! Before I listened to the live album, I decided to take a break, to take stock of what I had, to fully familiarise myself with Max's output, then I would approach the live album as if I were actually going to experience a Max Webster concert. A real-life experience that I would never have. The next best thing would have to do.

The playing of 'Live Magnetic Air' had been 'called off'... for now!

it's a wild party (live)

Discovering 'Live Magnetic Air' (1979)

The devouring of the three albums, and the rest of Max's back catalogue, took up plenty of my time over the next couple of weeks. I even managed to get one or two of my musician friends to begin to appreciate the genius of the band and Kim Mitchell in particular.

Incredibly, I had almost completely forgotten about my immigration application. Then one day, it arrived. I had been accepted, and I couldn't believe it! Here was an opportunity to change my life completely and forever. This news knocked me back a little because I realised, I wasn't sure whether I actually wanted to change my life.

Canada House simply stated, if I secured myself employment, they would issue me with a green card, which would enable me to live in the country for four years, after which, if both parties were satisfied with everything, I would be officially accepted.

I had a couple of employment offers; due to contacts I had made whilst over there. But I was unsure of which way to go. For now, I decided to wait. I didn't contact anyone in Canada, and kept the knowledge of the offer to myself, until I was sure of what course to take.

In the meantime (and the reason I was possibly having doubts about Canada), I was enjoying myself immensely. The band was still going great, work was still good, and time spent with my daughter Leigh-Anne, was wonderful.

She was a real handful, and we kept each other in our places. She grounded me. As it would turn out, she literally grounded me.

I was painfully aware that if I moved to Canada, Leigh-Anne would not be coming with me. Her home was with her mother and I would never have challenged that, even if I had been able to. 3,500 miles is a long way to be apart from someone you love.

Although I delayed making a decision, I knew in my heart what my final choice would be.

In the meantime, I did manage to get back to the North American continent, when I made a short visit to Manhattan. The city that never sleeps! That was a real experience. One I would recommend to anyone. Love it or hate it, I don't think there can be any in-betweens, everyone should experience New York and Manhattan Island at some point in their lives.

While there, I trawled through as many record stores as possible. It was here that I really began to notice for the first time, the diminishing numbers of vinyl records on sale. CDs were having a heavy impact on vinyl sales, and were beginning to take over! I felt like Kevin McCarthy in 'Invasion of the Body Snatchers'!

I was a die-hard vinyl supporter, and did not like this evolution at all. Where were the superb twelve-inch covers? Gatefolds? Double live albums? It felt as though a small part of me was dying.

This is where things go a little strange for a while. Whilst searching the record stores, hoping to find that golden enigma, 'Rockland' by Kim Mitchell, I came across something else. In the CD section, I came across a release by The Fixx, that I had never heard of, and... 'I Am a Wild Party (Live)', by Kim Mitchell!

I couldn't find the vinyl versions of either of these albums anywhere. I searched all over Manhattan in vain. I was to find out much later that vinyl versions of these records were never made.

It was hard to do, but I left the CDs, thinking I would find the vinyl versions in England. Boy, do I cause myself some work!

I never came across 'Rockland', in any format. Music wise, the trip had been a typical washout. But Harlem and the Apollo etc... Fantastic!

Once home, I had done my research, invested my time and bought my hypothetical concert ticket. It was my time to experience Max Webster live!

'Live Magnetic Air'! is undoubtedly a fine album. However, I do have one or two gripes about it. Let me explain what I mean.

The performances are exemplary. The choice of material is a good mix from the four studio albums, and it's full of obvious crowd pleasers. But, on a personal note, I love Max for the diversity exhibited on the studio albums, 'Words to Words', 'Diamonds Diamonds', 'Hawaii' etc, next to tracks like 'Beyond the Moon' and 'The Party', and then the rockers like 'America's Veins' and 'Here Among the Cats'.

I know that this small representation of Max live is fantastic! and that it's only a snapshot of the full show. But, why couldn't we have had the full show? A double album! No! Fuck it! A triple album? A band as complex, versatile and downright entertaining as this deserved a full live document.

I'm sure Max's shows were full of the playful likes of the 'Sarniatown Reggae' introduction to 'The Party', which we get only a snippet of on 'Magnetic Air'. More of this kind of thing would have been wild!

On a production note, I'm afraid, that I also find the production a little dumbed down. It isn't, how can I put it, widescreen enough? There's a little too much bottom end. The guitars and drums needed to cut through more, especially the guitars. Which may have made the whole thing feel more live and alive?

Recently I managed to get my hands on a bootleg recording from a Canadian television broadcast of Max in Barrie, Ontario. It was recorded on the Universal Juveniles tour, and is called 'The Boogie Is Everybody's Business'. Despite being a bit rough and ready, a little too... raw, it's fantastic! Mitchell toys with the audience at times. Sonically, it blows your head off. A real live feel to it.

That aside, 'Magnetic Air' is great fun and is absolutely essential. Like I said, the band themselves were at the top of their game, and the performances are unbelievable. It's only the brevity and the production of the recording which I'm slightly disappointed in.

The packaging is great. Some superb shots of the band in action, Moon references and a couple of tremendous photographs of the band with Pye Dubois on stage. The whole family together, having a party. Priceless!

On a side note, the British version of this album was just called 'Magnetic Air' and was one half live, and one half a studio best of. The full live album is much better.

'She takes more whisky than I whine?' I don't think so.

inhuman conditions

Back in the real world, I had decided that immigration to Canada wasn't on the cards, at least not for the time being. I came to this conclusion despite the fact that things were changing in my life. I was facing redundancy from my work. Rather than see this as the perfect opportunity, and reason, for moving to Canada, I chose to stay close to my daughter and try singing as a full-time occupation.

I handed my notice in with the band, and started singing in the thousands of Working Men's clubs that existed in every town and city, the length and breadth of the country. I became 'Michael Fury', club singer extraordinaire!

Usually, I would perform with the club's own drummer and keyboard player. Other times you would be lucky and the club would have a full band. These musicians would read music provided by myself, and it was pot luck if they were any good or not.

At the beginning, it was fun. A challenge, but invariably, the musicians were at best, average. Sometimes just plain awful. I performed with my heart in my mouth most times, wondering at which point the whole song would collapse and fall apart. It's a wonder I didn't suffer panic attacks right on the stage, such was my anxiety at times. Even then, it's doubtful whether the audience would have noticed, as most were just waiting for the nightly game of bingo to begin.

Yet, the money was tremendous. Most Saturday evenings were £200 to £250, so I wasn't about to give it all up without a good reason.

For me, the hunt for Max Webster material was over, or so I believed at the time, so the search for Kim Mitchell was back on.

Déjà vu! Where to begin. 'Rockland' and 'I Am a Wild Party (Live)' were both out there, somewhere, and there were two copies that had my name on them.

Other superb music had continued to seep my way from Canada through the 1990s; in particular 'The Tragically Hip' and the 'Rheostatics'. Canadian music, unfortunately continued, to be vastly overlooked and underrated internationally. Both of these bands deserve to be revered globally, not just in their homeland. And there are many other examples.

A friend of mine was going to London to visit his girlfriend, who had just started University. He went with a small shopping list. Three albums (I also wanted the Fixx album) all had to be on vinyl, naturally. I had faith, as he was a collector as well. The only downside was that he wouldn't be back for about a month. So, I had to be patient and concentrate on my singing career. Yeah. Right!

This was pure cabaret we're talking about here. Definitely no room for any Mitchell or Max. In fact, as I remember, the heaviest I managed to get away with was Bryan Ferry's 'Let's Stick Together'. If I ever tried to perform something the musicians hadn't heard of (they were, supposed to be reading remember) it was always a total disaster. Honestly, I still break out in cold sweats when I think of what some of those dreadful musicians put me through!

In the end, I started to introduce my own backing, in the form of pre-recorded tapes. This also enabled me to introduce material that the average audience wouldn't have a clue about. Although I enjoyed these songs, in the long run, it didn't work. Not only were the punters uninterested, they voiced their opinions, and if I wanted to be re-booked, I had to give them what they wanted. So, for a little while longer, out came the Elvis and the Beatles songs.

This went on for almost two years, but it was soul destroying. 'Musical prostitution' is how I thought of it. This was way before any smoking bans in this country and for a singer, the conditions were horrendous. One smoky club after another. And it was as lonely as hell. Friends didn't want to come and see you because they didn't like it either!

Eventually, I would realise this was not the reason I had started singing. I started because I had wanted to be Rob Halford or Bon Scott or even Bryan Ferry.

I eventually gave my agent a month's notice and started looking for a proper job. And a band.

If someone had told me where I would end up as a result of that course of action, I would not have believed them. I couldn't have believed them! To this day, it still surprises the hell out of me!

Even the thought of it was 'beyond the moon'!

purest gold

Discovering 'Rockland' (1989)

My friend returned from London with the distressing news that both the Fixx album and 'I Am a Wild Party (Live)' were unavailable on vinyl. He had asked at one of the stores and been informed that only CD versions of these albums had been released. It seemed like such an insignificant announcement at the time, but it was one that was going to change my life forever.

What he did bring back though, was a big fat twelve-inch vinyl version of 'Rockland' by Kim Mitchell; the follow up to 1986's masterpiece 'Shaking like a Human Being'. Glory days! Glory days!

Quite a few changes in the Kim Mitchell camp for this one. On drums we had Lou Molino. Bass guitar duties were by Mathew Gerrard. And on keyboards we had Greg Wells and Kim Bullard. We also had programming by Pat Mastelloto – how things were changing in recorded rock music...

I have to admit to being a little disappointed in Paul Delong's absence from the drum stool, but I needn't have worried on that score.

Along with the familiar and comforting presence of both Pete Fredette and Pye Dubois, the band had not just been changed, but expanded. And expanded was exactly what we got. This album was the Kim Mitchell band in widescreen.

The album is produced by the master himself and is, without doubt, the best produced album I have ever had the privilege of hearing. If only we had had the courage to contact Mr Mitchell when we were recording and self-producing our own album! If only! Mind you, he would have had to do it for about $50, and have paid his own expenses and his own airfare. We can dream!

The album begins with orchestral synthesiser, and then Pat Molino and Mathew Gerrard begin a clean uncluttered bass and drum rhythm and we're into 'Rocklandwonderland'.

You know straight away that Mitchell's production here is off the chart. It sounds phenomenal! The guitars, layered and multi-tracked, sound crisp and clear. The separation between instruments is sublime, and all are played to perfection.

A simple enough track with a 'straight forward' message from Dubois. It has a southern, sort of ZZ Top kind of groove, and is just fantastic! Mitchell's solo is blistering but sweet. The backing vocals from Fredette, Wells and Floyd Bell are powerful and angelic. Choir like!

I have a dislike of tracks that fade out, I feel that it's a bit of a cop-out and the artist obviously couldn't think of an ending. 'Rocklandwonderland' does fade, but there really is no other way to end this track, plus the fade sounds fantastic. Setting us up for track two perfectly. 'Rocklandwonderland' is faultless!

'Lost Lovers Found' is a love song. Blatantly a love song. As are one or two more tracks on this album. The band make no apologies for it, and why should they? There is nothing wrong with love songs within the rock genre. And the songs here, 'Lost Lovers Found' and 'Tangle of Love', are amongst Kim Mitchell's greatest achievements.

'Lost Lovers Found' is simply magnificent! Slow and brooding it is, once more, a production masterpiece. Its uncomplicated time signatures, a trade mark for most of this album, allow the song to wash over you and float you to places you could only ever dream of. A dreamer's song, in every sense of the word.

Mitchell's guitars are crisp and clean. Gerrard's bass work is sinuous and strong. Fredette works his vocal magic perfectly. Just a wonderful, wonderful song. Once heard, its majesty stays with you for a very long time.

'Rock 'n' Roll Duty' is more familiar Mitchell territory. Reminiscent of 'Akimbo Alogo' material like 'Lager and Ale' and 'Go for Soda'. A crowd pleasing, bar room stomping rocker which went on to be a concert favourite. Molino begins to let you know just what he's capable of here. His drum fills are fast, clever and precise. There's nothing too taxing with the song. The lyrics are purest Dubois. A great song! It lifts the mood of the album after the first two, calmer tracks.

For track four, we are back in mournful territory for what is for me, the album's masterstroke; the sublime 'Tangle of Love'. I'm not sure if Mitchell would agree with me on this one, I know that more than a few fans wouldn't. As far as I'm aware, it's never been attempted in a live setting. To be honest, it's probably not that suited to Kim's usual 'Rah Rah Ole!' type of concerts.

A very unusual arrangement, it is all about texture and feel. Another beautiful Pye poem delivered with intense passion by Mitchell. The lightness of touch displayed by the band here is astonishing. And I know that I keep going on about it, but the production is second to none.

Side one ends with 'Moodstreet', perhaps an apt, alternative title for the album? A strange track, which feels out of context with what's gone before. A little lightweight? It is, never the less, a good song, and superbly presented. But the album is of such an incredibly high standard that this and a couple of other tracks do tend to get overlooked within the bigger picture.

Interestingly, for some reason, the vinyl version of this track simply fades out, whereas the CD version has an unusual coda, which surprises right at the end of the fade...

I have no idea why. Perhaps the available space on vinyl was less? Welcome to Kim Mitchell land?

The return of Kim Mitchell, after a three-year absence and up to now, what a return. This was easily shaping up to being my favourite Mitchell solo album. I turned the record over!

That last simple statement, has profound meaning for me. You see, apart from replays of vinyl albums I already had, 'Rockland' would be the last vinyl album of Kim Mitchell's that I would ever buy. After this, it would be CDs all the way.

I didn't realise it then, but that turning over of the record signified the end of an era. Sad times!

'The Crossroads' opens side two in an up-beat, good time, feel good fashion. Wicked drum intro from Molino, synth bass, a la 'Shaking like a Human Being' and prominent 'choral' backing once again. Very commercial but ultimately, the kind of song Mitchell could write in his sleep. On anybody else's album a sure fire hit I'm sure, but placed amongst this collection, and for Mitchell, it seems mediocre...?

'Expedition Sailor' is a wonderful song in its own right, but at this stage, after 'Moodstreet' and 'The Crossroads', the album is crying out for a high-octane, mind blowing, unique arrangement of the type we're used to from Kim. As I said, it's a great song, lifted by a superb acoustic solo from the guesting Rik Emmett, from fellow Canadians Triumph. But once again, this is Kim Mitchell on auto pilot.

Any fears that the album's incredibly high standard was slipping is totally dispelled by the magnificent 'O Mercy Louise'. Pure Max Webster styled histrionics. Sheer gold! It rocks like a mother! Bizarre arrangement, great Pye lyrics and a peculiar mid-section, which is reminiscent of 'Miss Demeanour'. A fantastic song, great fun, and a saving grace for the album.

By penultimate track, 'This Dream', we are completely back on track with the album's early brilliance. Guitar driven rock, signifying the albums return to harder places. Mitchell's guitar work is playful and grooves as it does on the albums opening track, 'Rocklandwonderland'.

It would appear that the record had been on a journey, from harder times, through gentler pastures, and was now coming full circle. A great vibe here and Mitchells vocal delivery is vibrant and strong.

The album closer is the weird and wonderful 'The Great Embrace'. Reminiscent of 'Akimbo Alogo' material, like 'Diary for Rock 'n' Roll Men'. The band ends the record in storming fashion, including some of Dubois superior lyrical offerings. Out and out rock, with the usual quirky Mitchell/ Dubois touches. Superb!

As throughout this record, the backing vocals are an integral part of the overall sound, and are all over this track. Sounding magnificent, I might add.

Magnifique! Mitchell was obviously changing from album to album, and there were no signs of his creativity or standards slipping. Was there anywhere, a better collection of musicians assembled, time after time? It made you wonder where this astounding artist would go to next. In the short term, the answer would be live! Which caused a problem for me.

There were no more Mitchell vinyl albums to collect.

I didn't own, nor did I want to own, a CD player. Did this mean I had to stop?

But... 'juveniles don't stop', do they?

kim'r in action

Discovering 'I Am a Wild Party (Live)' (1990)

I was a vinyl record collector. I was stubbornly anti CD as I believed they had only been created to make as much money as possible for the record companies. With their bloated price tags, and the prospect of consumers having to buy products they already had in order to play them on their state-of-the-art CD players. Record companies stood to make an absolute fortune, again!

New technology in the music industry also had the profound effect of stifling the growth of any new talent throughout the 1990s. Companies were much less willing to take a financial gamble on an unknown artist as they were able to make millions on repackaging and reselling Led Zeppelin's or Pink Floyd's back catalogues. Without realising it, the late '80s saw the end of talent being given the time to nurture and grow. A sad day for us all. Music - and the music industry - would never be the same again.

To continue collecting, I had to diversify. Was it finally time to drag myself into the modern digital age? The end of the vinyl era? Should I make a stand for what I believe in? Or swallow my pride and embrace the new dawn?

Sod it. I bit the bullet!

I couldn't find the 'I Am a Wild Party (Live)' CD locally, so I contacted a friend in London, who worked in the city centre, and asked him if he would purchase and send me two CDs.

A few days later, they arrived. The first CDs I had ever bought.

As I've said before, you always remember the first time you saw, bought or experienced a thing. My first ever 7" single was 'Dark Lady' by Cher in 1974. I was only eleven and besides, it's not a bad song... is it? My first album was 'For your Pleasure' by Roxy Music, in 1973. To add to the list of musical firsts were my very first CD purchases. 'One Thing Leads to Another', a greatest hits album by The Fixx, and I Am a Wild Party (Live) by Kim Mitchell.

My first reaction to Kim's live album, after the cover (which I really like) was... It's short! So short! Only eight tracks! And for a live album, it turned out that only six of the tracks were actually live. What was going on? Had someone overheard my moaning about the short duration of 'Magnetic Air' and decided to rub salt in my wounds?

For the CD age, this seemed like an incredibly short number of songs, but when I played it, I learned this release was all about quality, not quantity. The master had done it again! This is a fantastic album.

This time around, the drums are taken up by Greg Critchley for the live tracks. With Lou Molino only appearing on 'Go for Soda'. The great Pete Fredette takes over bass duties, whilst still performing those amazing acrobatic vocals. Just check out his performance on 'All We Are' here. Like myself, you will be lost for words.

The overall live sound is phenomenal! It's electrifyingly exciting, making the listener feel as though they were actually there! The crowd levels are spot on, in fact, it rivals the best of the seventies double live albums era! Albums such as 'Live and Dangerous' by Thin Lizzy, 'Strangers in the Night' by UFO, 'Kiss Alive', 'Judas Priests', 'Unleashed in The East'... 'Wild Party' matches all of these for sound quality and intensity. A fantastic job! I would have preferred it longer, but... I know, I know. Shut up already!

The two new tracks on the album are both outstanding. The drummer for these is Matt Frenette, another superb addition. Where does Mitchell find them?

The CD... hold on a minute! I'm a life long vinyl lover so I'll continue to refer to them as albums. Ok?

The album opens with the first of the studio tracks 'I Am a Wild Party', a track Kim had been performing for a number of years prior to this recording. It was already a crowd favourite, and it's easy to see why. With its call and response chant of "Rah Rah Ole", it's rip-roaring stuff. Rocky, playful, humorous, downright action packed. It has everything that a great Kim Mitchell song should have. These are also Pye Dubois' best lyrics for some time.

'Deep Dive' is more brooding and serious. A powerful, mid-tempo rock song, which takes a few listens before you begin to fully appreciate it. An unusual 'bluesy' approach for Mitchell, but it works. A great song and a great album.

I knew at some point, I was going to have to see this guy perform in the flesh, so to speak. If he wasn't going to be coming to Britain, which looked doubtful, it meant only one thing, a long overdue return to the Canadian 'Great White North'. For now, that wasn't going to be possible. I had a full diary for my own live performances, which covered almost a two-year period. I wasn't moaning. This was great news, at least monetary wise; but the solo work was still continuing to depress me. I was beginning to get itchy feet about a return to Canada.

Life has a way of surprising you, time after time. Just as I was getting accustomed to the fact that I couldn't return to Canada anytime soon, Canada came to me. Completely out of the blue, I got a phone call from my old friend Rick from Montreal, although, he wasn't in Montreal, he was here! In Lancashire, and I would be seeing him within the hour. It felt as though a little part of me was coming home.

There must have been something 'in the stars' that night!

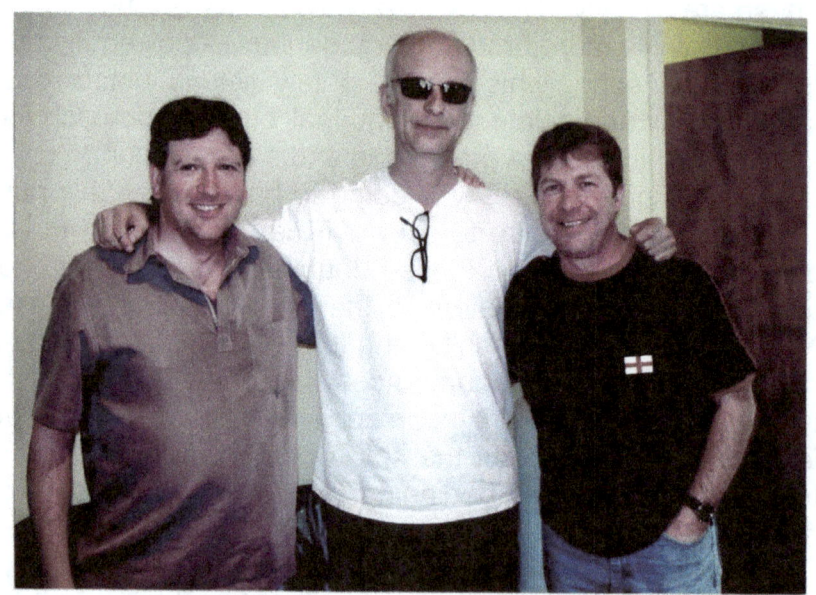

PETE AND MICK MEET KIM MITCHELL AT THE ALERT MUSIC OFFICE

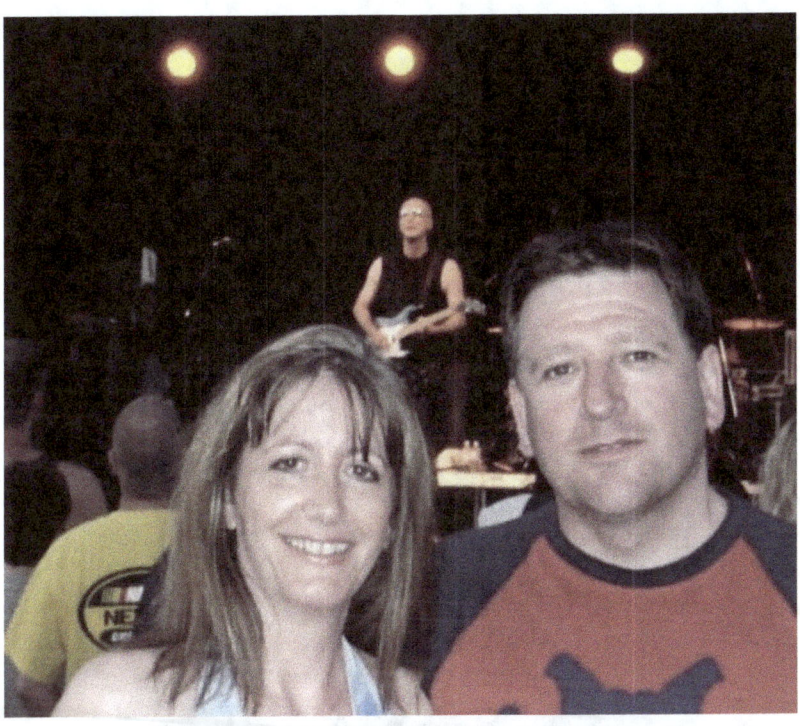

PETE AND ANN WATCHING KIM MITCHELL AT STRATHROY

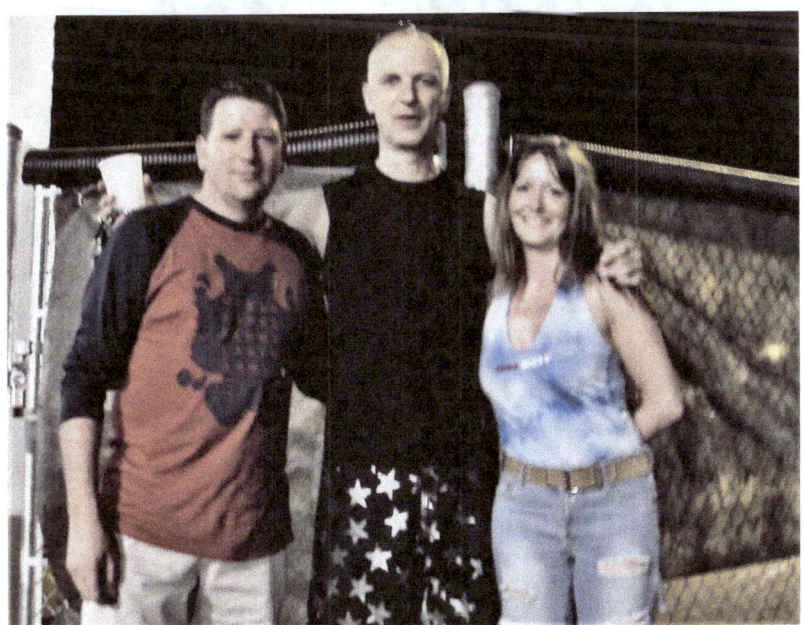

PETE AND ANN WITH KIM MITCHELL AT STRATHROY

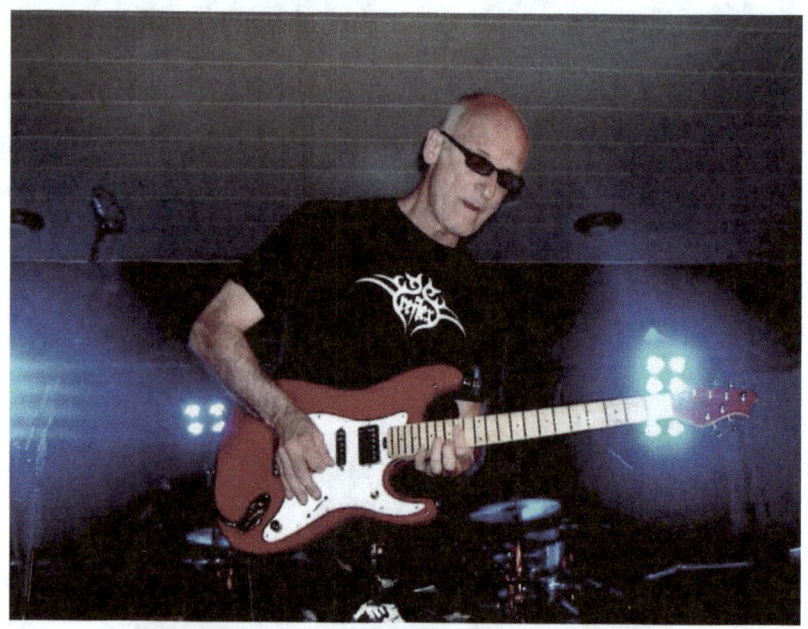

KIM MITCHELL AT THE BELGIUM CLUB IN DELHI, ONTARIO

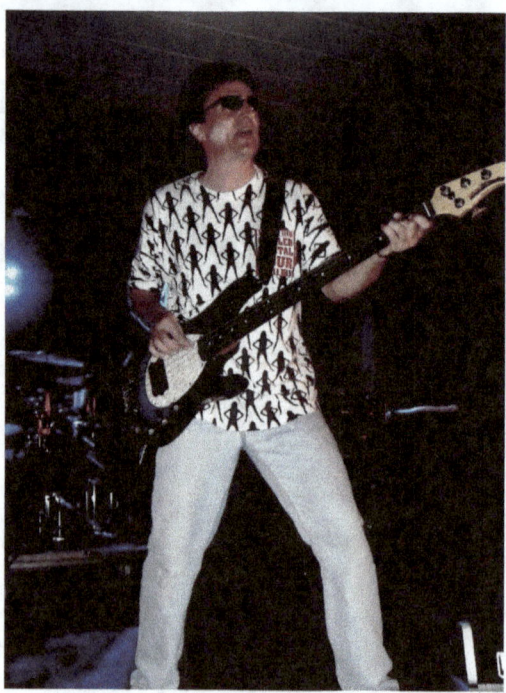

PETE FREDETTE AT THE BELGIUM CLUB IN DELHI, ONTARIO

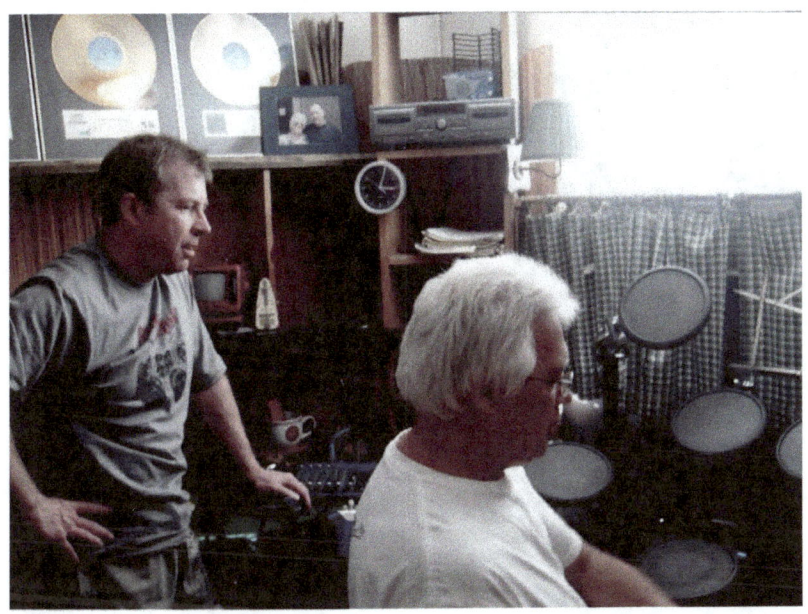

MICK HAVING A DRUM LESSON WITH GARY MCCRACKEN

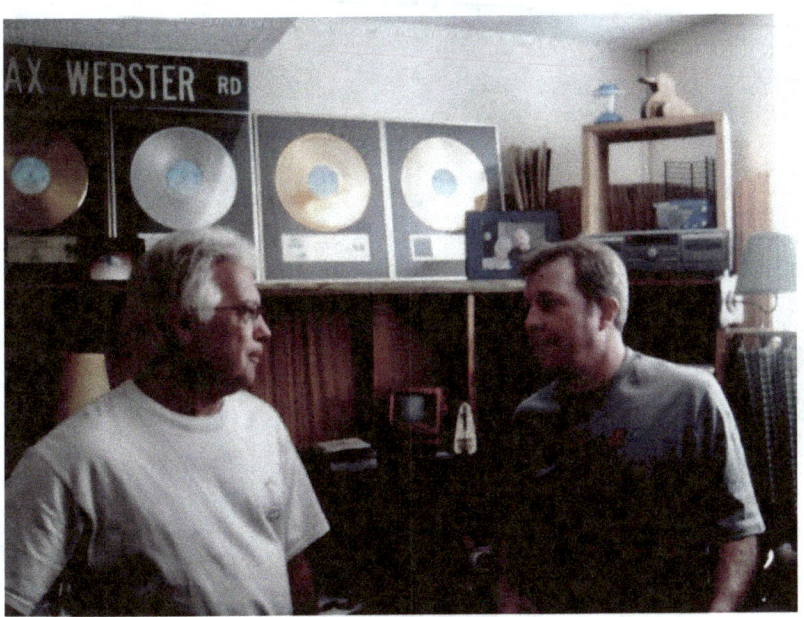

MICK WITH GARY MCCRACKEN

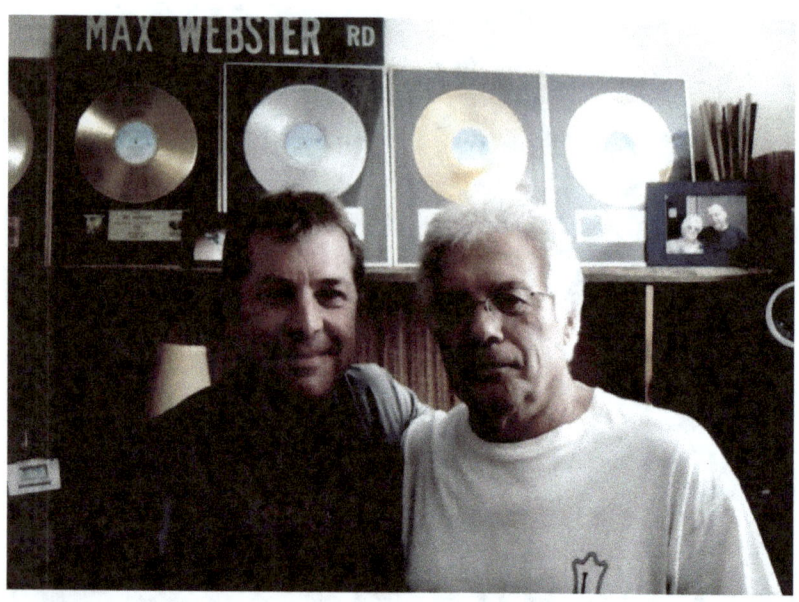

MICK WITH GARY McCRACKEN

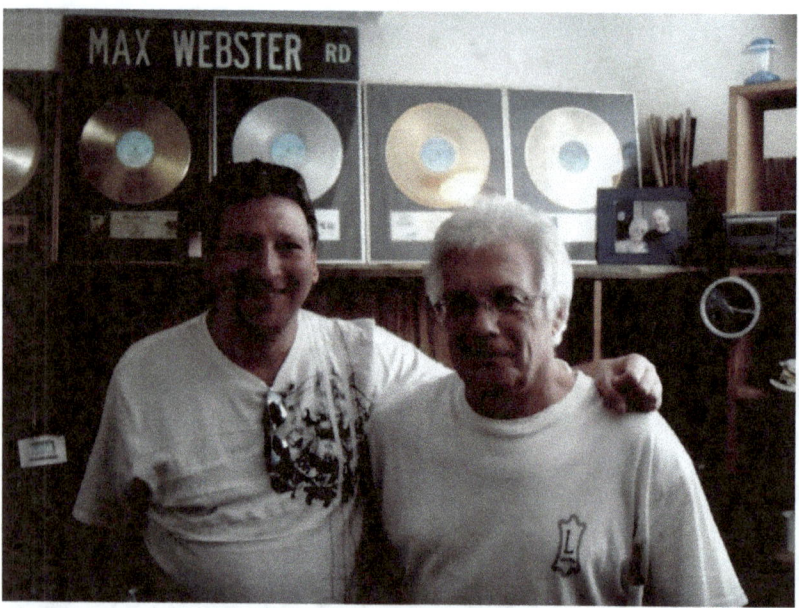

PETE WITH GARY McCRACKEN

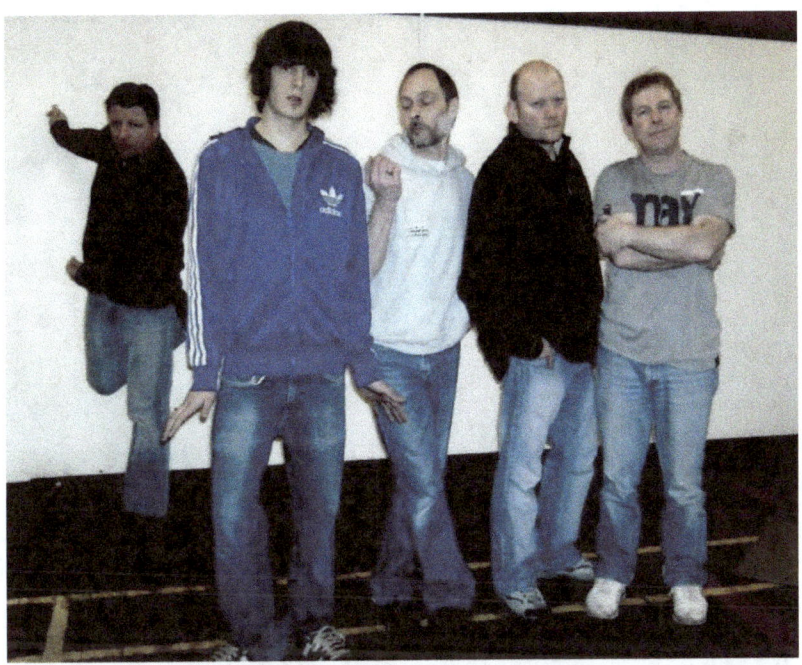

THE UNIVERSAL JUVENILES POSE FOR THE ALBUM COVER

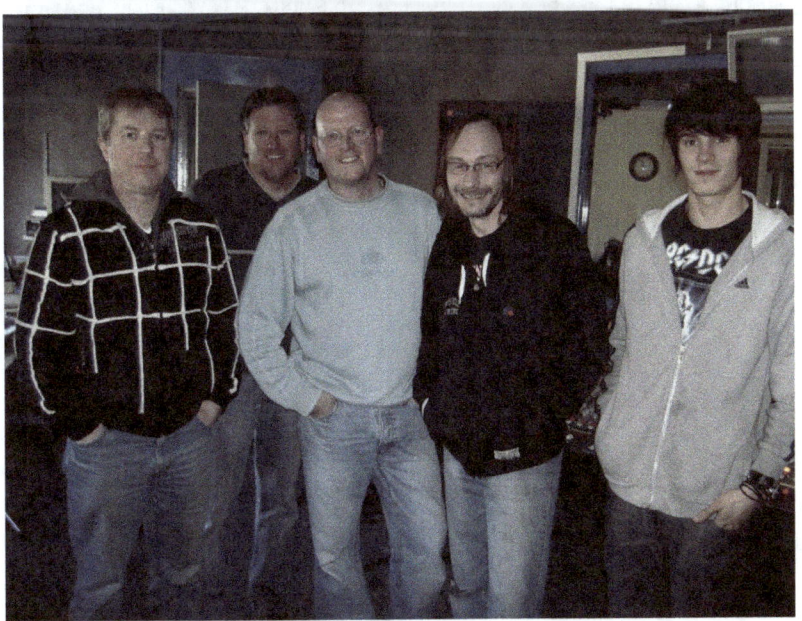

THE UNIVERSAL JUVENILES AT STUDIO STUDIO

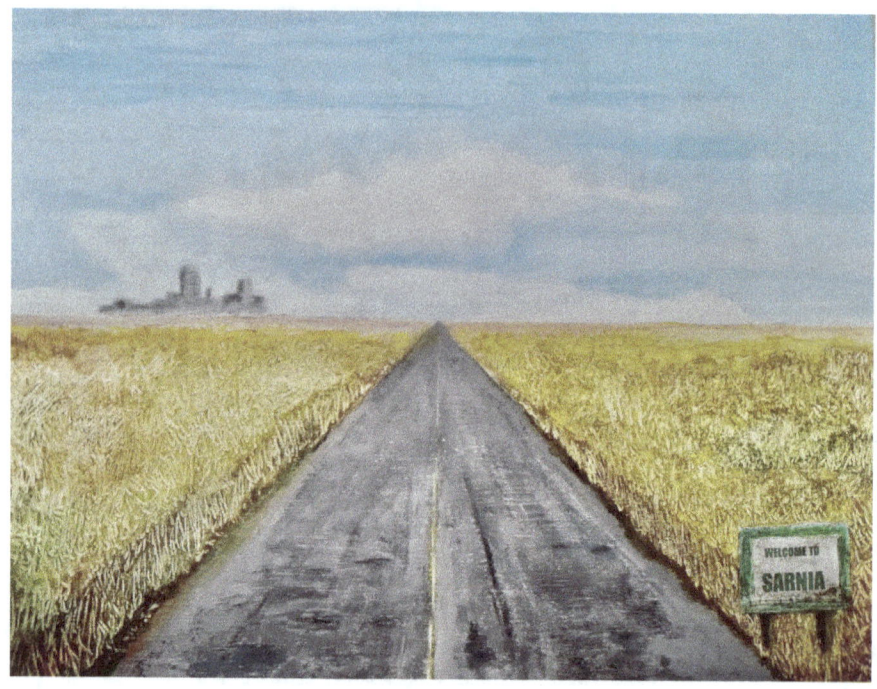

A PAINTING BY JIM HULMES OF A FICTITIOUS ROAD TO SARNIA, MAX WEBSTERS HOME TOWN

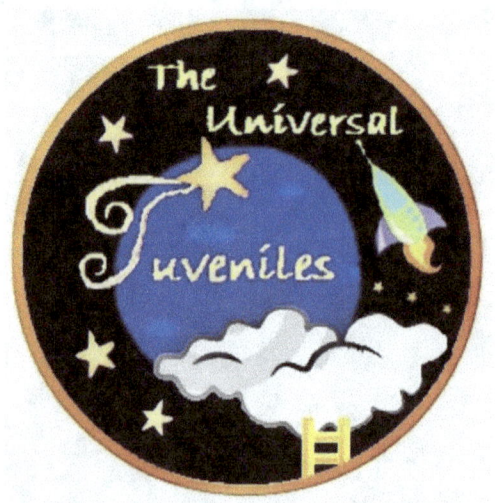

A LOGO FOR THE UNIVERSAL JUVENILES CD BY HANNAH WILSON

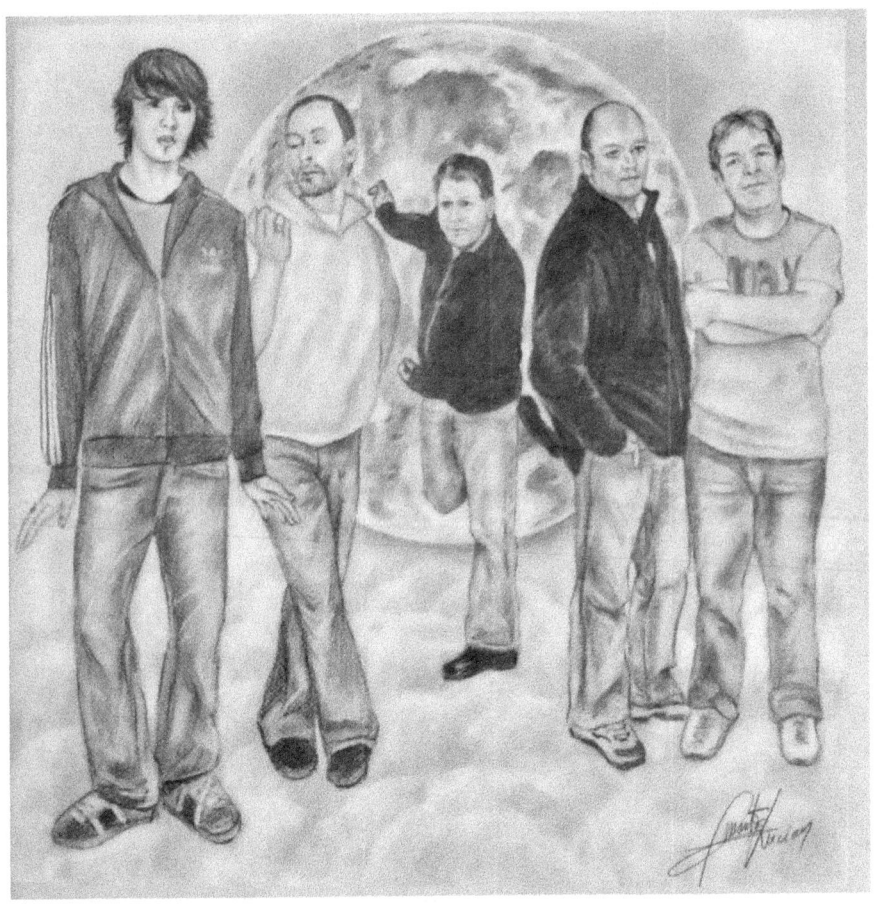

A RENDERING OF THE UNIVERSAL JUVENILES FOR THE CD COVER BY LUCIAN MANTOC

rumour had it

It was always great to see Rick again. The geographical distance made it so that we didn't see each other often enough. He had this strange Canadian/north England kind of accent which, the longer he spent in a northerner's company, would begin to sound predominantly more English with every passing sentence. He still does it. It's pretty funny.

He was telling me that he no longer lived in Montreal, and was living in Pickering, Ontario. During our conversations, it was apparent that the seeds of my return were well and truly planted. I just had to bide my time. He saw me perform as the ill-fated 'Michael Fury' and, although he was always appreciative of what I did musically, I could see that he also wondered what the hell I was doing. Mr Fury's days were definitely numbered.

Along for the ride with Rick was a friend of his, Jim Hallam, a doctor who had his own dental practice in Kitchener, Ontario, where he also resides. Over the years, I've got to know Jim well, and am honoured to count him amongst my friends. I had always thought that you would have to be kind of weird to want to be a dentist. I mean, who wants to look inside peoples' mouths all day long? Even for the money? But, after knowing Jim for over twenty five years now, I can tell you that my first assumption about dentists is 100%... correct! Weird! Only joking. Or am I?

Jim is also an avid record collector, mostly British music, funnily. When he learned of my Kim Mitchell fixation, he informed me that Mitchell had a new album out, 'Aural Fixations'! he thought it might even be a couple of years old when he told me. I also vaguely remember him stating that he'd heard it "wasn't very good"! But what would he know? He was a dentist for god's sake!

I quickly did some maths. Rick and Jim would not return to Canada for a couple of weeks, and then there would be a couple of weeks to find the album and send it to me, and then a further couple of weeks for it to arrive. Six weeks. Six weeks? Far too long for a Mitchell junkie such as myself. Instead, I had a cunning plan.

I telephoned A&A records on Yonge Street in Toronto, and asked them if they would send me the album, which was only available on CD. No problemo! they said. I obtained a banker's cheque in Canadian dollars and sent it off. Recorded delivery.

I anticipated its arrival so much that the rest of my friend's visit passed in a blur. Before I knew it, they were at Manchester airport and in the air. For a short time after, there was a hole in my life. One that I hoped, I would soon fill with the imminent arrival of 'Aural Fixations'.

"Imminent"? That was a laugh! I waited for weeks and weeks. I visited the post office and they confirmed that my letter had been received at the other end, but I could get no response from A&A records by telephone or letter. I was at a loss as to what to do.

At some point around this time, I had my 'wake-up' moment regarding my Michael Fury persona, and I packed it all in. Fortuitously, this coincided with my old band 'Thin Ice' searching for a new singer. Although I had no intentions of re-joining the band full time, it worked in both our favours for me to join them while they auditioned new singers. I ended up being back with them for almost a year. The timing could not have been more perfect.

One Saturday, I attended a record fair which was basically a huge second-hand vinyl market. Whilst there, I got talking to a Canadian store owner. I told him of my 'Aural Fixations' dilemma. He then dropped a bombshell. He told me the rumour was A&A records had gone bust. Liquidised. Gone into receivership. Whichever way you looked at it, someone had my money and I wouldn't be receiving my album anytime soon. I felt shell-shocked. Stunned. Traumatised! What was I to do?

I did the only thing I could do. The only thing that any sane person would have done. I applied to become a police officer in the Greater Manchester Police Force. Straight up! The idea came, completely, from left field!

Don't get the wrong idea. I did not think joining the police force would better equip me to locate my missing copy of 'Aural Fixations'. I did it because, well... I was tired of bumming around. I had a daughter and I had her future to consider. If I wasn't going to be a rock star, I wanted to aim for a decent career. One that both myself and my daughter could be proud of.

Knowing that the whole recruitment procedure could take up to ten months, I filled out my application, sent it off and tried to get on with my life the best I could. Trying not to be too distracted by what I was attempting to achieve, which was a monumentally life-changing career move.

All I could do was watch this 'space'!

all we were

Discovering 'Aural Fixations' (1992)

There were around seven stages to being accepted as an officer with Greater Manchester Police (GMP). The first was the application form itself. Over thirty or forty pages, they wanted to know the inside and outside of a cat's arse, as we say over here. They wanted to know, and have proof of, my school exam results. Now, whilst at school, I wasn't particularly academic, and as I had already secured an apprenticeship before my exam results were issued, I never bothered to find out my results. Now, sixteen years later, I needed to find out how many, if any, GCSE O-levels I had achieved, and send the paperwork to GMP. Where to begin?

The only thing I could think of as a starting point was to visit my old high school. I called in at the school office and told them of my predicament. At first, they said as it was so long ago, they would have no records available. I thanked them anyway, adding that it was my own stupid fault for not collecting them.

"Oh! You didn't collect them?" asked the secretary. "Just hang on a minute."

She turned and opened a tall filing cabinet, rifled through a few papers, and handed me my exam results! Sixteen years old, a little yellow around the edges, but all present and correct. I could have fallen through the floor.

I won't go into what exactly my academic achievements were. Pride will not allow it. Suffice to say, I passed this first phase of the police recruitment stages without any trouble.

Next up was the physical followed around six weeks later, by the physical fitness assessment. For a thirty-five-year-old, I surprised myself and passed, fairly comfortably. I was immensely proud of myself. I was half way there, and began to feel as though this could actually be more than a pipe dream.

Things were really going my way this time. The gods were, without doubt, smiling down upon me as one morning, without fanfare or rhyme and reason, 'Aural Fixations' arrived on my doormat from the now defunct A&A records.

Opening the package tentatively, I gazed upon the strangely interesting illustrated cover picture, created by Don O'Neil. It's a great cover, but... if only it had been on a 12" album. CD covers are just not the same. New artists, when looking upon their debut releases, can't possibly have the same feeling of euphoria that artists in the vinyl era must have had upon viewing their first LP or single.

Because it was a CD, I had a sad feeling of loss upon receiving 'Aural Fixations'. More so than when I obtained 'Wild Party', for some reason.   Oh well! Onwards and upwards, as they say.

Other great losses here was the horrifying absence of Pye Dubois. I scoured the credits, over and over, thinking I must be mistaken, or that it was just a dreadful omission. But no, Pye was AWOL!

This time around lyrics were provided by Jim Chevalier, Andy Curran and Moe Berg. Andy Curran, previously of Toronto band Coney Hatch, returning a favour here, as Hatch's debut album was produced in fine style by Kim Mitchell a decade earlier.

All in all, there were a lot of changes in the Mitchell camp for this one. Greg Critchley, who appeared on 'I Am a Wild Party (live)', keeps his place, understandably, whilst the bass player carousel continues with the addition of Ken 'Spider' Sinnaeve. The ever-reliable Pete Fredette, along with Rob Bertola, provides stellar backing vocals. Keyboards are provided by John Webster, a great surname for this story. Webster also co-produces the album with Kim Mitchell.

Quite a variation after the mega success, both artistically and critically, of 'Rockland'. I had no fears whatsoever about Mitchell's expert recruiting credentials. It was clear that he was not interested at all in hanging on to the past. I was worried about Pye Dubois' absence. This would be Kim's first album ever without his writing partner. I was also slightly confused by Mitchell's need for a co-producer. After all, 'Rockland' was my choice as one of the best produced albums of all time. But, never judge a book... as they say. Particularly when we are talking about Kim Mitchell. The proof of the pudding would be in the music.

'World's Such a Wonder' is a 'storming' opener. Driving bass and drums... loud, chunky guitars. Mitchell's vocal is on top form, and his slick lead work is bright, fluent and precise. The song breaks down towards the end, making the whole sound loose, spontaneous and alive. Reminiscent of his debut EP, it's a superb opener, showing anyone who doubted, after 'Rockland', which had its critics, that he can still rock out with the best of them.

A total change of mood for the second track, the smooth radio friendly 'Pure as Gold'. Superbly produced, and performed to perfection. Is it however, a touch too much middle of the road? A stunning guitar solo helps lift it above the average but lyrically, the first signs of the hole left by Dubois are displayed here. A good song though.

Next, we seem to be back on the right path with 'Big Smoke'. An out and out blues wig-out! Very simple and direct, but performed with immense power. Superb vocals again from Mitchell and the backing of Fredette and Bertola. The song sounds like it was great fun to perform, with Critchley's tight snare keeping everyone in check. The song appears much shorter than its six-minute duration.

Production wise, the album was shaping up to be a magnificent affair once again. A tighter feel to 'Rockland' in that the band appears live and less produced. More stripped back. The backing vocals are further back in the mix and, overall, you get the impression of a live band in action, not session musicians in a studio. Stirring stuff'.

'America' is for me, the album highlight. A fantastic song. A funky, bouncy riff with a slight country vibe. Mitchell is on tremendous form for these sessions, both vocally and guitar wise. The songs are full of clever, incidental touches on the strings. Subtle but inspired. The arrangement for 'America' is brilliantly constructed, fairly straight forward, but it builds dramatically. Lyrically, it is also the best offering after 'World's Such a Wonder'.

By this point, you feel as though we are on for a real winner, but 'Some Folks' slips us back to 'MOR' land. Almost, dare I say, Bryan Adams territory? Don't get me wrong, these are great songs, and the band is phenomenal, but I'm not sure if Mitchell was purely searching for hit singles here, and stopped writing from the heart. A good song, adored by women everywhere, I'm sure. And maybe it could have been a hit. The lyrics by Chevalier, are direct and custom made for a potential hit. But this isn't what I expected, or wanted, from Kim.

I was missing Pye Dubois. I thought Kim Mitchell and the band, were missing Pye Dubois. 'Aural Fixations' was a long album though, twelve tracks, so two or three average songs would be far from a disaster here. I just hoped and prayed that we weren't entering into Michael Bolton land.

'Find The Will' restores faith. A rock song with a return to Kim's occasional southern inflected boogie. The lyrics are stronger, as is the overall performance. A song which would not have been out of place on 'Akimbo Alogo'. The band sounds as though they are having fun again. Looser and playful, unlike on 'Pure as Gold' and 'Some Folks', where they sound restricted and sapped of energy.

So, half way through, and up to now we'd had four great songs and two good (but average songs). Average for Mitchell's standards, that is, on a superbly produced and performed album. All in all, things were ok! What would the second half reveal?

'There's A Story' has a brooding synth intro, then we move into comfortably familiar Mitchell terrain. Chevalier's lyrics, after 'Pure as Gold', are improving and fit Mitchell's format here much more comfortably. Musically it is guitar driven heaven, a real feel-good song, which has a 'Shaking like a Human Being' feel. A funky song with a great instrumental section. One of the album's best songs.

'Dreamer' threatens to slip into schmaltz land at first, but manages to retain Kim's deftness of touch and uniqueness throughout. Reminiscent of 'Patio Lanterns', it's pure Kim Mitchell, and a much more appropriate attempt at the charts.

Next up is the rip-roaring 'Dog and a Bone'. A good time, bar room stomp! AC/DC would be proud of the riff Kim conjures up here. Out and out rock. The rhythm section of Critchley and Sinnaeve pound the song along like a freight train. Wonderful!

It appeared as though my consternation caused by a couple of earlier songs on this collection had been, well and truly, banished. 'Aural Fixations' was fast becoming another superb offering. Add to that the tremendous live sounding production (well done Kim and John Webster) and one or two experiments, with three songs to go I felt it was, already, hats off time to the master.

'Flames', unfortunately, just does not do it for me. Similar to songs he would later explore on 'Kimosabe', it misses the mark, as it were, and just sounds syrupy and weak. There is possibly, one of the best guitar solos ever recorded during the song but even that can't save it. Remember though, this is just my humble opinion, and I'm sure 'Flames', 'Some Folks' and 'Pure As Gold' each have their fans. Deservedly!

The album ends in magnificent style with the final two songs. 'Hullabaloo' lives up to its name. Another great riff which leaves plenty of room for the band to play around in the spaces. Tremendous fun, and the band sound spontaneous, almost like a jam session recording. Just what music, and the Kim Mitchell Band, should all be about.

An unusual move for Mitchell with the album's finale, but an inspired one. The record ends with the guitar extravaganza instrumental 'Honey Forget Those Blues'. A jazz/blues tune which just lights up the room. Written solely by Kim, he nevertheless incorporates five guest guitarists to help him perform this one. Rob Piltch, Mike Francis, Bernie LaBarge, Jim Taite and Bobby Edwards who also arranged the composition. The choral guitar work sounds like a big band brass section which, I'm sure, was the desired effect. It works tremendously well and ends the album on a glorious high.

A very good album, and a brave first step for Mitchell without Pye Dubois. Mostly superb, with just a couple of songs that I'm still unsure of but I have to admit, I missed Pye, and hoped that the separation was only a temporary one. Time would tell and unusually, I didn't have to wait long at all to find out.

Things were happening 'fast and furious' for me around this time. I felt as though I was 'hitting the ground' running!

paradise pye

Discovering 'Itch' (1994)

The police recruitment procedure was going really well. I had successfully completed five out of the seven assessment days. I had managed to detach myself from any anxiety over the selection process, as I had always presumed that at some stage, I would be unsuccessful and subsequently rejected. With two assessments left, rejection was still a possibility of course, but now, being so close, it began to feel more and more like a reality rather than fantasy. At this point, the nerves began to kick in a little.

The assessment days were always in Manchester, and after a particularly satisfying conflict resolution assessment, I made a trip to the city centre to browse through HMV and Virgin. I made my way straight to the 'M' section and pulled out... 'Itch' by Kim Mitchell. I was absolutely stunned. I hadn't even known of its existence. Things were definitely going my way. Deciding this was a good omen, for the first time, I was confident that I would actually become a police officer.

Driving home, I have to admit I couldn't figure out the title of Kim's new album. For a time, I thought the album was just called Kim Mitchell, not realising that the 'itch' from 'Mitchell' was the actual title. The cover is good, with a multi-armed Kim itching and scratching and with mosquitoes also present on the cover it's hard to see where my initial confusion came from. Perhaps it was the pink colour scheme chosen for the album? Who knows?

Any confusion of the album's cover, title or colour scheme is totally irrelevant once you start to play the disc. Simply put, 'Itch' is without doubt, Mitchell's best album since 1986s 'Shaking like a Human Being' and one of the best albums of his career. I would even include his time with Max Webster.

Produced with magnificent raunchiness by Joe Hardy, the album is classic Mitchell. Personnel wise, the Kim Mitchell band is a trimmed affair here. Basically, a three piece of Mitchell, Spider Sinnaeve on bass and Greg Morrow on drums, augmented by Lou Pomanti on keyboards, with backing vocals from William C. Brown III, Bertram Brown and Pete Fredette.

The big news though, was the triumphant return of Pye Dubois. Put out the bunting! Unfurl the flags! Fanfares all round! Wonderful, wonderful news!

The album opens with the hard rock blast of 'Wonder Where and Why'. Hardy's production here gives the guitars a looser sound; almost Rolling Stones-like. It's a great touch, one which Mitchell and the rest of the band thrive on. The song is relentless, never pausing for breath. It's a great introduction, and by the time of its conclusion, the listener is as breathless as the band must have been after this superb take.

Greg Morrow's cracking drums snap us into the grungy 'Acrimony'. All hail the return of Pye Dubois! This is a fantastic lyric. Biting, but also very funny. A superb comedic observation on middle/lower class trials and tribulations. The arrangement is varied and shocking; unsettling, but in a good way. There's a lot going on here, and it leaves the senses confused and numb! Pure Max Webster. In fact, this album could have easily been the sixth Max Webster album. That's a compliment, obviously.

'Lick Your Finger' is a dirty, bluesy rocker. Still with a Stones feel, it nevertheless conjures up images of the

'Mutiny Up My Sleeve' era Max. A simple enough rocker, it is sheer, feel-good boogie.

After the explosive opening three songs, 'The U.S. of Ache' is a timely respite. A slow and mournful love song and one of Mitchell and Dubois' best ballads of their career. 'Ache' is the operative word here. The song, the performance and the listener's heart all ache during this performance. The only things that don't are the ears. Beautiful lyrics, and Mitchell's guitar is sweet and clean. The unobtrusive keyboard work from Pomanti is a glorious touch, and fills out the song magnificently. A wonderful, passionate creation. Paradise!

'Lemon Wedge' is just plain Barmy! A bizarre construction, which is tremendous. A fun-filled, funk-fest, right up there with 'Toronto Tontos' from Max Webster, and 'Rascal Houdi' from 'A Million Vacations'. As I've said already, this whole album has echoes of Max all over it. An absolute joy!

This was not only shaping up to be Kim's best offering for some time, it could also be argued that 'Itch' was Pye Dubois' career high. Maybe creatively, he needed that break around 'Aural Fixations'. On 'Itch', it was clear that his batteries were fully charged. For proof of that, look no further than 'Heartbreakbustop'.

Not only a great title, Pye, once more, displays how cleverly he can twist the meaning of a word to something totally different. "Calling it off, before we get on" indeed! 'Heartbreakbustop' is a mid-tempo rocker. Meaty with a great groove and superb backing vocals. Ending the first half of the CD in tremendous fashion.

I was overjoyed, everything was back in place. Disorder in the universe had been restored. I played the first six tracks a few more times before progressing, and totally fell in love with the album. Everything, so far, was so good that it almost didn't matter how good the second half would be. 'Itch' was already a masterpiece!

'Your Face or Mine'. Southern boogie at its best with an added Status Quo vibe. Pure fun. As you can guess from the title, although it is a great blues/rock song, it's not meant to be taken too seriously. It's just the band and Pye throwing pretensions to the wind, cranking it up and having a ball!

'Human Condition' finds Mitchell and Dubois in an unusually sombre and reflective mood. A ZZ Top kind of boogie. Almost like a slowed down 'Acrimony', it's a biting indictment on society's selfishness. Deep and serious. A heavy, riff-based song with metal leanings. A powerful song.

'Stand' is simply superb. Lightening the mood considerably, it bounces along at a gallop. An extremely uplifting experience, it would have fit seamlessly onto Kim's debut EP. Strangely, whenever I play this album, I can't help feeling as though 'Stand' would have worked perfectly as the album's closing track. It leaves you on a high, and is basically a hard act to follow. Classic Mitchell!

Thankfully, it wasn't the last track and there's plenty more to come on this wonderful collection.

Remaining in the good time zone, 'Karaoke Queen' is a rousing, bar room pleaser, which must have had them dancing in the isles at concerts. A surprisingly heavy song at first, for such a light topic. It does however, brighten and lighten for the fist in the air, sing-a-long chorus. Superb!

Shock to the system time with penultimate track, 'Cheer Us On'. An acoustic, campfire song. Deftly played on twelve strings, with tasteful vocal backing. It's a moving and heartfelt song and it, successfully, leaves the listener with a sense of loss. Beautiful! As a standalone track, it is simply stunning, but doesn't really fit with the rest of the album, and sounds slightly out of place.

The album ends with the quirky 'Beachtown'. A harmless bit of fun with a definite Max Webster feel to it. A good song, but perhaps a little throwaway after such a monumental collection of songs. I believe that 'Stand' would have made a better closing track.

What can I say? A superb album! Kim Mitchell was back, firing on all cylinders, with the indispensable Pye Dubois by his side. I couldn't stop playing this album, cranking it up in the car whenever I got the chance. It became the soundtrack of my life for the next few months, spurring me on in my endeavours and eventually, accompanying me into the Greater Manchester Police, as I was finally accepted into the force.

For the first time I felt genuinely anxious. I really did feel as though little old me was entering into 'the world of giants'. Scary!

hard times

It had taken almost a year of hard slog and total commitment. I can't describe my feelings of euphoria upon receiving my letter of acceptance. I had a few weeks to get my affairs in order before I reported for duty. Albeit, at the training college. I only hoped that I wouldn't make a fool of myself as I reported to my senior officer. Somehow, I was sure that "P.C. Hulmes reporting for Rock 'n' Roll duty, sir!" would not go down too well with my superiors.

Joining the police force involved a two-year probation period. This involved six months' worth of residential courses, or 'modules', which were spread out over the two years. I have to admit, I found it all incredibly hard going. It was a total change for me. The discipline, the competitiveness, studying and physical regime all took their toll on me, both physically and mentally. I was also quite a bit older than most of my 'classmates', so at times I felt out of place socially. I found it difficult to adjust to my new way of life.

What was also making my adjustment difficult was that Manchester has a huge police force, which is kept incredibly busy by the city's large population. I had been stationed at one of north Manchester's busiest sections, Collyhurst.

Whenever I returned to the training school, I invariably found that most of my other colleagues were still to make their first arrest, even though we were fast approaching the first anniversary of our recruitment. For them, this allowed plenty of time for studying and socialising, and I could see certain individuals progressing in leaps and bounds in their adjustment to the police way of life. I, on the other hand, found myself back-classed at one point, not because I was falling behind on my studies, but because I had to spend two weeks at Manchester Crown Court, as I was the officer in the case (OIC), for two counts of robbery and two counts of blackmail.

The files I had to create on these cases were immense. I was making upwards of ten arrests per week, and I hadn't been in the job a year yet. The time spent away from the police college were the reason I had to be back-classed. This was demoralising and I was also becoming exhausted. But I was here! I had made it and was still incredibly proud of my achievement.

Everyone who joins the police, at some time or another, questions whether they have made the right choice. I was certainly no exception, but nevertheless, I was determined to persevere and succeed.

On a lighter note, it was around this time that my brother Jim, announced that he would be visiting Canada for a work conference. He would be stopping in Barrie, Ontario, a place I had visited in 1983, but didn't know well. He would only be in Canada for a week or so, but said he would be spending some time in Toronto. Inevitably, I gave him a small note. On it were a couple of addresses where he might be able hook up with a few friends but more importantly, I gave him a list of Max Webster and Kim Mitchell albums that he was not to buy – as I already owned them - but he was to pick up anything else not on the list he might come across.

Thinking back, it's strange that my brothers visit to Canada didn't stir up more emotion in me than it actually did. I was obviously too wrapped up in my police situation to really think about anything else.

Confident that I had everything by Mr Mitchell, I put any thought of surprises from Canada out of my mind. Imagine, then, my astonishment and pleasure upon my brother's return, when he handed me Kim Mitchell's 'Greatest Hits'. With further inspection of the compilation, it became apparent that there were four new songs on the album, plus a version of 'Expedition Sailor' which I didn't have, which was referred to as 'the other version'. Intriguing!

The packaging was great but didn't contain a great deal of information. The actual cover gives tantalising images from videos, which obviously exist, but I had never seen. I found this very tormenting at the time. The three portraits enclosed of Kim are also really good, and successfully reveal the humour within the artist.

The collection is excellent, a wide range of material and a fine selection. One or two missing that I would have included but that's always going to be the case with a 'Greatest Hits' compilation. You can never please everyone.

The new songs are all superb. 'No More Walking Away', co-written with Dubois, is an unabashed love song. Nothing too outstanding, but performed to perfection, it completely hits the mark. Heartfelt and yearning, it makes you wonder what Pye was going through in his private life when he wrote this. Mitchell's vocals, as always, are exceptional.

It was unknown at the time but 'No More Walking Away' would, ironically and sadly, be the last time Mitchell and Dubois would collaborate on a song together. Sad news, which went unnoticed at the time.

The new recording of 'Lager and Ale' follows, and it's a storming success. Not particularly better than the original, but it is surprisingly harder and much raunchier, therefore very different. If this was the desired effect, then it succeeds admirably. A fantastic version.

'Rainbow', co-written with Andy Curran is, for me, the better of the two truly new songs. A funk rock song, it grooves like a mother! The lyrics are good, and the arrangement is clever, with a few twists and turns to surprise us. Similar to early Kim Mitchell material like 'Tennessee Water'. A great song!

The new version of 'Patio Lanterns' is a laid-back acoustic campfire song, performed in a style similar to 'Cheer Us On', from 'Itch'. It's ok, but not a patch on the original. It is fun though, and I'm glad that this version is out there. Anything 'new' from Mitchell is a blessing, after all.

The 'greatest hits' throws up a couple more oddities. The aforementioned 'Expedition Sailor' (The Other Version), is a strange arrangement of the 'Rockland' classic. Extended, but not really of any benefit from the original. A touch more choral backing vocal, and Rik Emmett's acoustic solo seems to be more prominent in the mix, as does the synthesiser but, apart from that, it's pretty similar to the original. Nice to have a different version though.

At the beginning of the live version of 'All We Are' there is an unusual, isolated track recording of the opening synthesiser motif. Weird and quite possibly, unnecessary.

The album is book-ended by the short sample tracks, 'Transcendental Soda' and 'Hare Soda', which are recordings of the crowd from 'Wild Party' repeatedly singing 'Go for Soda'. A nice touch to an excellent greatest hits package.

The album was quite timely for me as it accompanied and helped me through the residential periods of my police probation. Most times taking my mind of the stresses of constant work and study.

As I began to approach the end of the probation period, I began to feel as though I was getting more to grips with the whole situation. The actual police work was getting easier to handle, as all the knowledge I had to retain began to sink in. The studying side of things was now coming fast and furiously, but even that was now beginning to feel easier.

My life was about to change as very soon, I would qualify as a police officer and I also said goodbye to the band 'Thin Ice', as they had now found a new singer. One of my last performances with them was at the police training college, so that had been a nice moment for me and, I hope, for the band too. It also meant that, for the first time in my adult life, I was not in a band or looking for a band. I thought that my singing days were behind me. At least for the foreseeable future. Little did I know!

I also bought a house with my girlfriend of five years, Denise, and, as it was my seventh home in as many years, I decided to sell my record collection! Three thousand albums were a lot to be moving around so repeatedly and, having already bought a few CDs, I thought I would sell, and then replace on CD, my records. I kept a few that I wanted, until I actually had their replacements. Max and Mitchell were amongst these few. Now, the hunt was on again to find the CD equivalents of all those amazing albums.

Everything in my life was just about falling into place when... disaster struck! Whilst on duty during a routine call, I was attacked by three adult males, all of whom were high on some drug or other. The attack put me in the hospital and, from that moment on, my future as a police officer was placed in jeopardy.

'Cold reality' or what?

battle /carred

The attack happened on a gloriously hot summers afternoon. I was half way through my shift when we received a call from communications of a threat of violence. When I and my partner arrived at the scene, there was a fight in progress between three males, there was a knife on the ground with blood on the blade and one of the males was bleeding from his throat. Upon our arrival, they immediately refocused their aggression on us. I was the first in the firing line, as it were, and was attacked next to the police car. Neither my baton or the CS gas spray had any effect, as they were high on drugs. The gas, however, did affect me and, within seconds, I was blinded.

The whole 'battle' lasted around seven minutes before back-up arrived. The side of the police car was completely smashed in, with the wing mirror ripped off. But, more seriously, after examination at the hospital it was discovered that I had damaged thirteen vertebrae. I could hardly walk. After a few weeks off, I returned on recuperative duties, and began months and months of physiotherapy. From what the doctors were telling me, it seemed that it was touch and go whether I would recover sufficiently enough to carry on my career.

Having just bought a new home these became incredibly stressful and worrying times.

Eighteen months after the attack, I was still under the medical officers' supervision and still on recuperative duties.

This meant that I was working nine to five, Monday to Friday, instead of shifts. It was office work, collating and inputting stop and search information into computers. Relevant, but mundane and boring as hell! I was still getting paid, but every morning I found myself questioning my existence as I put on my uniform. I was depressed and emotionally scarred.

Every time I visited the doctor, I went in putting on an act that I was fine, but I couldn't fool him, and each time I hoped to be returned to full duty, he knocked me back. Fuelled by the uncertainty of my future, I could feel my depression getting worse. Determined to not let it get the better of me, I did something that I had wanted to do for years. I contacted some friends, booked a month off work, and booked a trip to Canada!

It had been a staggering thirteen years since my last visit. For me, it still felt as though it were only yesterday that I was converting the church into a nightclub on Kingston Road, going to watch the Argonauts at the exhibition centre, or walking along the boardwalk in the Beaches. So much had happened to me in those thirteen years. It was easy to see how I had not had the time to return to Canada, even though I had wanted to so many times.

I contacted Rick, who was still living in Pickering, and he was more than pleased for Denise and I to stay at his place for the three weeks we had planned.

Once the flights were booked and we started to plan the holiday, I began to get really excited. For the first time in over a year, I was enthused about something. I felt like a child approaching Christmas day. We were going to be visiting Niagara Falls and Niagara on the Lake, going to concerts, one in particular I hoped, visiting friends I hadn't seen in years and a football game, as it would be right in the middle of the CFL season. We even planned a road trip to Vermont, via Ottawa and Montreal.

I was determined to fit in everything we possibly could, including my search for Kim Mitchell concerts and CDs remember. My back was feeling good, and as long as I didn't do anything too strenuous, the doctor said the break would be good for me, physically and more importantly, mentally. I think the doctor had begun to see the lines of worry, stress and depression appearing on my face.

Before we were due to leave, I received some good news about work. When I returned after the holiday, they wanted me to become part of the drugs investigations team. I would still be office based, but the work would be far more interesting and rewarding than what I had been doing for the past twelve months.

Things were beginning to look decidedly brighter for me. I was going to have a fantastic holiday and for the first time in ages, I would actually be looking forward to going back to work. But that was a whole month away.

Canada! The great white north! It was time to 'let your man fly'!

toronto pronto

Approaching landing at Pearson International Airport, we circled over Toronto in a bright and clear blue sky. I could clearly see Lake Ontario, sparkling in the heat. The islands, the three black towers of the Dominion buildings, the bank of Montreal, the CN tower, rising above it all, and the Sky Dome, which was new to me. Incredible memories came flooding back; I could hardly contain my excitement. Anticipation had been eating away at my insides for the whole seven-hour flight. Thirteen years, but I was finally here again.

Rick picked us up from the airport and we hugged like brothers. One thing I always notice whenever I visit Canada is its big sky! It is just an unusual anomaly and a stark contrast coming from England, with its constant low ceiling of grey clouds. Ontario, with its flat expanse of terrain and its typically clear cloudless sky, is a pleasant shock to the system.

We arrived at Rick's late in the afternoon. He'd arranged a few drinks at the house with one or two friends including his dad Winston, whom I hadn't seen since 1986. Winston Beckett, could you get any more English? The evening passed in a blur. I got royally drunk and, although it was six in the morning for us, we managed to stay up until around one in the morning.

The next day, bright and early... ok, around lunch time. I put the first part of my plan into action. I got Rick to go on the internet and check out when and where Kim Mitchell might be playing. He logged on and I had two terrible cataclysmic shocks. According to the internet, Kim Mitchell had "no planned concerts at this time". I was absolutely gutted. I couldn't believe it. Wouldn't believe it, so I got Rick to search further. I wish he hadn't.

It transpired Max Webster reformed and toured Canada just last year. I kept reading this information over and over, as if doing so, I might get transported back a year and be deposited in the front row of a Max extravaganza!

It didn't happen of course. As I write this, I can still feel the disappointment I felt at missing the band by one year and the anger at myself for not using the internet more. I'm such a technophobe! Only one day into the three-week holiday, it felt as though it was already over.

I was despondent for a couple of days, but I was in Canada, I had a million places to go and people to see. My spirits lifted considerably when I saw that we had arrived just in time for the start of the CFL season. The Argos' opening game was to be against their old rivals Hamilton, the team I had seen beat the Argos in the eastern final, thirteen years earlier. This was a game I wasn't going to miss.

We walked to the train station on lakeshore in Pickering, and the train took us to Union station in downtown Toronto. The journey was fantastic. Although I hadn't taken the train along the lake to downtown previously, the experience felt oddly familiar. As Toronto's skyline drew steadily closer, my heart was in my mouth.

When we got off the train at Union, I immediately saw signs pointing the way to the Sky Dome along the Sky Walk. Intrigued, we decided to go and pick up the football tickets first and set off along the sky walk. What a view! Talk about being in the belly of the beast. I felt like Jonah! The buildings towered up around us, dwarfing us in their majesty. We were so awestruck at the view, the walk took almost an hour, as we couldn't drag ourselves away from that spectacular panorama.

The Sky Dome itself looked amazing from outside. I love all sports stadiums and had visited many over the years. I couldn't wait for the game in a few days-time. I had been told the stadium had a retractable roof. That would be a first for me. I entered the ticket office and purchased two tickets. They were handed to me in a small paper envelope. Without looking at them, I placed them in my pocket, and we began the tour of the city.

Of course, I wanted to visit all of the record stores along Yonge Street but Denise didn't really share my passion for browsing thousands of records, so I would just visit a couple of stores, and return another day to browse to my heart's content.

In the end, I only visited Tower Records on the corner of Queen Street and Yonge. I was thinking of buying as many Mitchell and Max CDs as I could find and afford during this trip but, astonishingly, I found next to nothing in Tower Records. The racks were devoid of Mitchell material. It was almost as though there was a boycott on selling his music. That's what it seemed like. All I found was a Max Webster compilation, 'Diamonds Diamonds', which appeared to contain two tracks that I didn't have. A little disappointed, although it was early days, I bought the CD and left. Pronto! I was pleased to have the two new tracks.

Downtown hadn't changed much. There was a lot of building work or demolition going on across from the Eaton Centre and I noticed a Hard Rock Cafe, which I couldn't recall seeing back in '86. Massey Hall was still there of course, and things looked very familiar. It wasn't long before I felt as though I knew my way around again.

Back at Rick's that evening, I was able to put on the newly acquired Max CD, and we had a few cold ones. Whilst listening and waiting for supper, the atmosphere was that of a party once again, so I didn't get much chance to really take in the new tracks on the CD. Instead, I decided I would get up early ahead of everyone else, make a coffee, and put the headphones on. And 'wave at my dad'? Perhaps not.

'Diamonds Diamonds' has a really cool cover. Snapshots of the band caught live and in studio poses, all spread over a psychedelic print of Mitchell onstage at a large arena. Again, the albums overall effect is probably much better appreciated on a twelve-inch cover, than on the CD.

The song selection is a superb cross section of the first four albums. The album was released in 1981 but, unusually, doesn't contain any selections from 'Universal Juveniles'. Going off the production credits, the two previously unreleased tracks, seem to have been recorded around the time of the 'Mutiny Up My Sleeve' sessions and are probably outtakes from the album. Although, this isn't made clear in the credits.

Both 'Hot Spots' and 'Overnight Sensation' do have the feel of 'Mutiny' material. With Terry Watkinson's piano high in the mix, 'Hot Spots' is a short and inoffensive slice of Rock 'n' Roll. Good fun but nothing outstanding, and it does sound a touch throwaway?

'Overnight Sensation' is of a similar ilk, but more like late '60s or early '70s rock. Good guitar from Mitchell and swirling organ from Watkinson. Surprisingly, although both written by Mitchell and Dubois, neither sound particularly like a Max Webster song. They also sound ever so slightly, under produced. Not quite demo material but... unfinished? Possibly discarded long before 'Mutiny Up My Sleeve's' final touches. Nevertheless, I am proud to have these two songs in my possession, which makes 'Diamonds Diamonds' an essential addition to anyone's collection.

It was still only around seven thirty in the morning. I was listening to the CD repeatedly, when I remembered the Argos tickets we bought the day before were still in my jacket pocket. I got them out and began to read the added information which was included with the tickets. Suddenly, I woke the whole house up! I couldn't believe my eyes, or my luck. I read it again, to make sure I wasn't mistaken, then I leapt from the chair, screaming and punching the air like I had just scored the winning goal in the World Cup Final!

Before the Argos/Hamilton game, there was to be a tail-gate party (a communal parking lot gathering before major sports events). Performing at the party, free of charge, would be... The Kim Mitchell Band!

Now... just think about that incredible slice of luck for a minute. What would you say were the chances of something like that happening? To this day I can't get over it. After thirteen years, I thought my search was finally reaching its conclusion. Little did I know that it was only just beginning.

This was turning out to be, one in 'a million vacations'!

live and desire

Friday 23rd July, 1999. 6pm Toronto time.

The tail-gate party, which is basically a drinking/eating get together before a big game, took place on a small plot of land just outside of the stadium.

We arrived very early, around three in the afternoon, in order to secure a good spot, and hopefully get a glimpse of Kim and the band before the show, which wasn't due to start until six. Who knew, maybe I would even get a chance to meet him, although that seemed like too much of a pipe dream at the time.

When we arrived, there was no one else there, just the stage and the road crew. I got talking to one of the crew who, unbelievably, originated from St. Annes, a Lancashire town not twenty miles from me. I found this incredibly strange but, understandably, he didn't really share in my incredulity. He informed me that Kim and the boys hadn't arrived yet, but should be arriving shortly for the sound check. Unbelievable! I was going to witness the sound check as well. Could the day get any better? We took our places on the empty concrete and waited for the chosen one's arrival.

About an hour into our wait, Denise announced that she needed to go and find a toilet as she was bursting. There didn't seem to be one around where we were, so I advised her that she may have a better chance of locating one at the stadium or at the CN tower. She set off in search, and handed me her jacket and handbag to look after while she was gone.

A few more people had started to arrive and I noticed one or two of them talking to someone at the side of the stage. Straining my eyes through the brilliant sunshine I saw that it was Kim Mitchell himself, live and in the flesh. He was talking and having his photograph taken with fans. I couldn't believe it! This was my chance. I leapt to my feet and started to make my way to the stage. Suddenly, I stopped and the realisation of my predicament struck me, smack between the eyes. Here I was, about to meet my idol, a god! All my recent hopes and ambitions came down to this one moment, and... I was carrying a lady's handbag!

I panicked. I turned my back on the stage, quickly hiding the bag. What was I to do? Approach him and hope that he wouldn't notice? Or that he might notice, but think it was a cool European look? No! Of course not! He would think I was a weird, lunatic Englishman, who carried a lady's handbag and would desire more than a handshake!

I had no choice but to sit and wait, handbag hidden, until Denise returned. When she finally did return, my moment had passed, and Kim was on stage, tuning his guitar. I did manage to get some good photographs of him alone on stage, but I knew that a real opportunity had, once again, slipped through my fingers.

The show itself was something else. Kim Mitchell live! I was right at the front, "Rah Rah Ole'ing" with the best of them. I remember it being incredibly loud. Phenomenal, but loud! My ears rang for three days afterwards. At one point, Kim was introducing a song from 'Itch', announcing that the album had only sold around five copies. I remember shouting out with pride that I had bought one. I don't think he heard me.

I made a mental note of the set list and, at the earliest opportunity, grabbed a pen and wrote it down, so that I could make a cassette tape recording of the songs in set order to play in the car when I got home. I still have the list and the cassette, even though I no longer own a cassette player. I know... sad!

The set was only twelve songs, but what a dozen. 'Rocklandwonderland', 'Easy to Tame', 'Lager and Ale', 'I Am a Wild Party', 'Lemon Wedge', 'Big Smoke', 'Acrimony', 'That's the Hold', 'Battle Scar', 'Patio Lanterns' and 'Go For Soda'. With 'Rock 'n' Roll Duty' as an encore. Seventh heaven! Cloud nine! Nirvana! It was fantastic. A concert experience I will never forget.

It was over far too quickly, and I never got near to the stage area at the end, so I didn't meet him. At least, not on that occasion.

The Argos played a great game. It was close, but they lost. That night, I looked down on the floodlit stadium, through the domes open roof, from the glass floor of the CN tower. What a day! One I won't forget. Ever!

As we made our way back to Pickering that evening, the concert still ringing in my ears, my feet didn't touch the ground. It seemed as though I floated 'in my cloud' all the way.

A 'dreamer' indeed!

on the roads

Over the next couple of days, and before the road trip, I managed to get back into the city to go record hunting. Well... CD hunting. I got up early and made the journey by myself so that I could browse without pressure or distraction. With the combined efforts of three record stores on Yonge Street; 'Sunshine', 'Sam's' and 'HMV', I managed to buy just four of the ten CDs I was looking for. A disappointing ratio really, but I was sure that given time, I would eventually find them all. After all, in a couple of days I would be in Ottawa and Montreal.

I had managed to find most of the Max Webster CDs, 'High Class In Borrowed Shoes', 'Mutiny Up My Sleeve', 'A Million Vacations' and 'Universal Juveniles'. There was no debut album or 'Magnetic Air' to be found. Surprisingly, I didn't find any Kim Mitchell solo albums. Was there a boycott on his solo work in Toronto? It certainly seemed that way.

The CDs were disappointing in that there was scant information included and the covers are spoiled by having the unnecessary advertisement of "featuring Kim Mitchell" emblazoned on the front. A poor marketing decision. The albums deserve much better treatment and are long overdue for a serious repackaging and re-release campaign. But I had them, and I was now armed with some serious listening material for the immense road trip ahead of us.

Loaning us his car for the week, Rick waved us off as we set off on the 260-mile trip along highway 401 to Ottawa. Due to being delayed by a spectacular thunderstorm, we arrived in Ottawa at nightfall. As we had planned to leave early the next day in order to reach Vermont, we never got to see Canada's capital city. We certainly didn't experience it. The little I did see, the parliament buildings, the river, the buzzing city centre, all made me sorry we were leaving so soon. I made a promise to myself to return one day.

We had decided to drive to a small ski resort town in Vermont, USA, which Denise had heard was a beautiful place. She was right, Stowe is gorgeous. It immediately reminded me of the town in Twin Peaks. Spectacular and friendly, I would recommend it to anyone. Interestingly, it also turned out to be the home of Ben and Jerry's ice cream factory and the place that the Von Trapp family (made famous by the movie The Sound Of Music) settled after the war. A great place to visit, but it had been an exhausting 240-mile road trip and... no record shops. Next stop would be Montreal, Quebec. Perhaps my last opportunity to complete my Mitchell CD collection.

We were reluctant to say goodbye to Stowe, and ended up leaving in the late afternoon. By the time we reached Montreal, we just had enough time to locate a cheap hotel, find a restaurant for an evening meal and then crash out. I had driven around six hundred miles down many roads and all driven on the 'wrong side'. I was exhausted!

The following day, our only full day and night in the city, we crammed as much in as we could. We visited old Montreal and the cathedral. Viewed the city from atop Mont Royal and even went out to the Olympic Stadium. But we saved the city centre, and the record stores, for the evening.

It was sweltering that evening, so all I put on was a T-shirt, shorts and sandals and we set off to walk into the centre. After buying five CDs in Toronto, Denise had laid down the law that I wasn't to buy any more. Not only that, but I wasn't to go into any record stores and spend hours perusing the merchandise. Of course, if the opportunity arose, I was going to have to ignore these 'demands'. Things were not going too well though. As the evening progressed, as pleasant as it was, I found myself having to walk past record store after record store. Time was running out. I needed my 'fix'!

My chance came when Denise announced that she needed to go to a chemist and that she also wanted to have a look at a couple of clothes shops too. Being the caring, unselfish person I am, I suggested that she should take her time, and I would meet her in a half hour back at the bar that we had just been in.

The major record stores were just too far away for me to make it in time, but I had seen a smaller independent store just a block away. I hot-footed it back to the store. It turned out to be my saviour. Apart from Mitchell's debut EP (which I found out later was not available on CD), the store had all the albums I was looking for! Max's debut, 'Live Magnetic Air', 'Akimbo Alogo', 'Shaking Like a Human Being' and 'Rockland'. Five CDs! I wanted them. Needed them. But, if I bought them, how would I conceal them from Denise? all I was wearing was a T-shirt and shorts. A bag would have been the sensible solution, even a brave solution, but it was out of the question, I wasn't that brave. There was only one thing for it, I bought the CDs, bundled them together, and placed them inside the front of my shorts. With my T-shirt pulled down over my crotch. As long as I didn't make any sudden movements, the CDs were, surprisingly, fairly well concealed. Dancing would be out of the question, though.

I took my place at the bar, standing, and waited for Denise to join me. The CDs were digging into my thighs and were very uncomfortable. When Denise arrived, she suggested we take a seat. Panic stations! There was no way that I would be able to sit down. Impossible! Thinking on my feet, I said that I would prefer to stand, saying the beer always seemed to go down better that way. I got her a bar stool, she sat, I stood, and the terrifying situation balanced on a knife edge, which was how my balls felt after an hour or so of the CDs digging into me, passed without incident. Just discomfort.

I managed to get back to the hotel in one piece, and secreted my bounty into my bag. She never found out. Of course, all this secrecy and deception didn't bode well for our future together, and we broke up a few months after our return to England. It's sad when relationships end but, thinking back, I will always have my... CDs!

The car broke down on the 401 during the 330-mile return journey, perhaps hinting at a sign of things to come. We had to be towed the last few miles back to Rick's place. What a trip! Almost a thousand miles, three wonderful locations and a completed Kim Mitchell collection.

The holiday had been fantastic. And I had, finally, seen Kim Mitchell live! Saying goodbye to Rick, I promised him that I would return as soon as I could. I certainly wouldn't be leaving it for another thirteen years to pass. As we flew out of Toronto that evening, I knew that I had left another small piece of myself behind, once again. Wiping a tear away, I vowed to return very soon in order to collect it.

I remember that particular journey across the Atlantic as being a long, depressing 'night flight'.

a crossroads

Discovering 'Kimosabe' (1999)

Police work plodded on for a few more months upon my return, but the end was nigh! As expected, I was deployed to the drugs unit, but later I was transferred to the incident room to work during a murder investigation. I now had good reasons to drag myself out of bed each morning. The work was interesting, exhilarating and thoroughly rewarding.

Unfortunately, on one of my numerous visits to the police medical officer, he had dropped the bomb-shell that, in his professional opinion, my injury would never repair itself sufficiently for me to continue my duties as a police officer. I was given a further two months until my next examination. I began a fitness regime that was as intense as I could manage in order to get myself fit to resume duties, but I was less than confident.

As the end was approaching, two amazing things took place for me. Firstly, I managed to see the superb Tragically Hip at the Shepherd's Bush Empire in London on their 'Music at Work' tour. They were stunning! As an added bonus, they were supported by Sloan. Good, eh? More importantly though, whilst reading the small ads at the back of Q music magazine, I came across an advertisement for a small record store that specialised in rock music. Amongst their new releases advertised was a Kim Mitchell album called 'Kimosabe'. I telephoned the shop and confirmed they had a copy in stock. I reserved the copy and, after work that day, I took a twenty-mile detour and took possession of 'Kimosabe', Kim Mitchell's first album of all new material since 'Itch' in 1994, a staggering five years earlier.

Back in my usual routine at home, I cleared the decks, got myself a couple of beers ready, and placed the disc in the player.

'Kimosabe' has a great cover, one of my favourites from the Mitchell catalogue. Cool, soothing colouring and with Mitchell looking older, wiser and introspective in the photographs. The photo of this version of the 'Kim Mitchell Band' shows them relaxed and informal, much like the music contained within. Mitchell returns to the producer's chair here, which is good news, but there is no Pye Dubois. Writing duties are, once again, taken up by Andy Curran, who previously contributed to 'Aural Fixations' and 'Rainbow' from 'Greatest Hits'. He also contributes fine backing vocals to the album.

The band is: Gary Breit on keyboards, Randy Cooke, drums, and Pete Fredette on vocals (obviously), but also on bass guitar. An accomplished bass player, this was nevertheless Fredette's first studio bass duties for Kim, having played bass live for the 'KMB' for some years. Other guests are; Carlos del Junco, harp. And the great Lisa Dalbello on vocals. A superb collection of musicians once more and in particular, Randy Cooke who is for me, Mitchell's best drummer since Paul Delong.

There was a lot riding on this album. Rumour had it that Kim financed the production of this album himself by re-mortgaging his home. Foolhardy? No! Just sheer simple dedication. And an absolute travesty on the part of the Canadian music industry.

The album opens with the stupendous 'Monkey Shine'. A statement of intent from Mitchell who, after five years away, may have felt he had a point to prove here. He didn't, but he proves it anyway. 'Monkey Shine' simply slaps you across the face and demands your attention. A guitar driven boogie, with plenty of humour both musically and lyrically.

Dubois himself would have been proud of this one. A very sparse presentation. Almost raw and similar to the sound achieved on Kim's debut. A good move after the mega production values of recent offerings like 'Rockland' and 'Fixations'. It allows the sheer talent of the band to shine through. Mitchell's voice is wearing well, and the power in his voice is amazing. He also pulls out all the stops with his tasteful guitar licks. Super!

'Stickin' My Heart' is a slightly different style from what we are usually used to from Mitchell. A rock song with country touches, it is fairly raw, with Cooke's excellent drums well to the fore. It's a good uncomplicated song arrangement, with another outstanding vocal from Mitchell, and has a great rhythm and a strong chorus. Good fun.

'Cellophane' changes the mood and slows things down considerably. A funky groove from Fredette's bass, which is subtle and danceable. Reminiscent of 'Miss Demeanour', you just can't keep your feet still to this one. With Breit's wonderful jazz inflected electric piano, the song is a pure delight, and one of the albums highlights.

Staying moody and low key, 'Two Steps Home' is the album's first ballad. It's a very personal sounding lyric, reaffirming Mitchell's introspective look on the cover shots. It's a superb, heartrending performance from all, but Mitchell excels here. His voice has never sounded so emotional, and his control is astonishing. Pop idol and X-factor contestants should take note here on how it should be done. There's no substitute for experience.

Lest we forget, apart from his vocal talents, Kim is also one of the world's greatest guitarists. 'Kimosabe' reminds us of that fact in fine fashion. A powerful and heavy, guitar driven rock song, with a beautiful sweet solo. Fredette's prominent vocal chorus adds another dimension to the whole album, growling and menacing. A strange and interesting atmosphere to end side one on, if CDs had sides. Thought provoking stuff! Moody and edgy. Wonderful.

'Blow Me A Kiss' is a light hearted, bouncy slice of fun, despite its misleading melancholic opening bars. Breit's simple, single note piano motif in the verses is a nice touch, counterbalancing nicely with the frenetic sing-a-long choruses. A feel-good number, which should have been a hit single. Ah! If only.

Now then... next up are the two songs that I can't quite make my mind up about. Mitchell was obviously going through a lot of turmoil in his personal life around the time of writing for this album, and both 'Cold Reality' and 'Over Me' are very personal songs. Both written solely by Mitchell, they lay the singer bare, as he found himself at one of life's many crossroads, and are emotionally from the heart. Acoustically built, they are very good songs, but for me, they are far too personal and hard to enjoy. Perhaps Mitchell succeeded too well in relaying his emotions at the time. The gift of a songwriter or the curse? It is not my place to decide.

Moving on, penultimate song 'Get Back What's Gone' is a lighter affair in more ways than one, as it's easy to envision cigarette lighters held aloft in concert halls all across Canada during this song. A stripped down, smoky night club blues song, with a strong vocal accompaniment from Dalbello and even harmonica (harp) from Carlos del Junco. A nice song, but fairly throw-away for Mitchell's standards.

What can be said about the albums final track, 'Skinny Buddha'? Simply put, it's 'Kimosabes' standout track, and one of Kim Mitchell's finest achievements of his career to date. It has Max Webster written all over it, and even has the trademark Mitchell weird guitar solo, of which he was most prolific of back in the Max days. You never know what's coming next here, as the song twists and turns unexpectedly. Incredibly strong vocal backing throughout, solid drumming, all go to make this a storming rollercoaster ride of an album finisher. Lyrically, as in most of the songs here, the song is humorous and good-natured. Despite Dubois' absence, this has been a stellar effort, and Andy Curran deserves praise for his work on 'Kimosabe'.

A great album, despite the odds stacked against it and the poor corporate backing, Kim Mitchell soldiers on. His extremely high standards showing no signs of a compromise. Kim has always produced high quality guitar and vocal performances but on 'Kimosabe', I think the balance shifts more to his voice? And what a voice. Roll on the next album!

Meanwhile, back in my world, I visited the medical officer for the final time. He knocked me back again, and I asked him to let me go, basically handing in my resignation. On paper, I was now retired from the police force on medical grounds.

Where to now? Unemployed and with a 'bad back'? It seemed that I was also standing at my own personal crossroads. I decided to try and re-join a band and start singing again. At the time, singing felt like the only constant in my life. An outlook that unexpectedly, was about to change.

I was about to get mixed up in the surprising 'tangle of love'!

found the will

My life took several turns in the right direction over the next few months. Firstly, I managed to get myself involved in a band again. It was hard going at first, although I would not consider myself old at 38, most bands that were advertising for singers were considerably younger than myself (as it should be) so I deemed these to be unsuitable. I found out that most musicians around my age either didn't care to do it anymore, or were already employed in working bands. Just as I thought about giving it all up as a bad job, I stumbled upon the fact that my new neighbour, Jason Steel, was a fabulous keyboard player and, as an added bonus, he was also a prolific songwriter. Together we formed a band called Electricgarden.

Predominantly, we performed '80s covers when we played live but, as a side line, we co-wrote many songs together, and even recorded an album called 'Tango of Life'. Although the album was never actually released, I'm still immensely proud of the album; the songs are strong and good and stand up well, even today.

At one point, and unbeknownst to me, Jason forwarded one of the songs, 'Astronauts and Racing Drivers', to the Eurovision Song Contest in the hope that it may be chosen for that year's British entry. Although it didn't win, it managed incredibly to make it into the top fifty out of thousands of entries. This resulted in BMG records being interested in us. Unfortunately, they eventually passed. For a short-time we thought our boat had come in!

I also found employment working for the Law Courts as a warrants officer, or enforcement officer. A great job, not too dissimilar to the police, and with good prospects. I really fell on my feet with this one, after the disappointment of my release from Manchester police, and I am happy to say that I am still here with them today.

I also returned to Canada, although this time around, I really wish I hadn't bothered. The omens for anything good to come from this visit were stacked against it from the beginning. For a start, I was due to travel in the same week as the 9/11 atrocity. For the whole week, I didn't know whether I would be flying to Canada or not. To be honest, after 9/11, I didn't care whether I flew or not. Along with anger, like many other people, I was gripped with apathy! It felt as though the world simply stopped spinning. Time stood still. Nothing much seemed to matter. The decision of whether I went to Canada again or not seemed trivial and pointless!

It transpired, surprisingly and suddenly, I was cleared to fly. I had a feeling of numbness as I travelled, almost as if it was an out of body experience. This was not solely due to the effects of 9/11, it was also because I was in the grip of one of the worst colds I had ever suffered. It worsened during the flight, probably due to the cabin pressure, and then again during my first week of the holiday. For seven days, I was virtually housebound.

As my cold eventually began to subside, I started to regain my appetite. Having hardly eaten a thing for the past week, I raided the fridge at Rick's. What I ate should have been thrown away about three weeks earlier. As I was recovering from my cold, I contracted food poisoning! What a holiday. For the next couple of days, I had 'stuff' coming out at both ends. When it finally subsided, I slept for two days solid!

All I can recall of this three-week stay is how I was determined to salvage something from it. During the last couple of days, I dragged myself to an Argos game. I can't remember who they played! I can't remember the score. I bought no records during the trip, and made no attempt, whatsoever, to see Kim Mitchell in concert. I still find it hard to forgive myself for these lapses in dedication but boy! was I glad to get home.

So... ok! A holiday to forget, but I was in a tasty little band and employed in a rewarding occupation. Things were looking good and I felt as though things could only get better. They sure did! I met and fell in love with Ann. Simply put, the best thing to happen to me since the birth of my daughter, Leigh-Anne. Amazingly, she fell in love with me, at least that's what she says, and she can't be with me for the money, so maybe it's true? Ann brightened up my world and together with my daughter, they are the two reasons why life is worth living. Kim might be the third reason, but don't tell my family or friends.

To express my feelings for Ann, I decided to take her to Canada, a place nearly as close to my heart as she was. It would be less than a year after my last trip. Ok, I was also eager to wipe away the memories of my last, disastrous visit and hopefully make amends for the Kim Mitchell free zone my last visit represented.

Rick had now relocated to Cambridge, Ontario, right on the opposite side of the city from Pickering and out in the sticks, but very close to our friend Jimmy in Kitchener. Getting to Toronto city centre from Cambridge is frankly, a bit of a nightmare. It's a long stressful drive. There is a direct bus, but the train is quicker, the only problem with that is a 45 minute drive to the train station. Oh well! Beggars can't be choosers, as they say.

Apart from finding out that Kim Mitchell was entertaining the undeserving westerners in Alberta and British Columbia during our visit, and we would therefore not get the chance to see him (I'm only jealous, people of Canada's western territories), this vacation turned out to be everything I hoped it would be. A return visit to Niagara Falls which this time, was not only dramatic but romantic as well. No. Rick didn't accompany us.

We did all the touristy stuff and included two outstanding concerts in our itinerary. We saw Aerosmith at the Molsen Amphitheatre, who were supported by Kid Rock and Run DMC. We also got to see The Tragically Hip play a benefit concert at Walkerton, a small town, around eighty miles or so north of Cambridge. At the show, The Hip were supported by Great Big Sea and The Watchmen. Both concerts were awesome!

At Walkerton, something occurred that will live with me to the day I die. The show ended at around ten thirty on a Sunday evening. Most people, perhaps twenty thousand, had parked their vehicles on the other side of the town from the venue; this meant that all these young people had to walk through housing estates to get to their cars, past homes where people had maybe retired for the evening in order to be fresh for work the following morning. I was absolutely amazed at the respect these thousands of youngsters had for their fellow man. No one spoke, unless in hushed whispers. A throng twenty thousand strong and the crickets were making more noise than the fans. I tell you, it would have been a completely different scene, and atmosphere, in broken Britain. I would love to live within a society that had such manners and respect for others. Just another example of why I return to Canada, time and time again. A beautiful experience!

Ann was also bowled over by what happened after The Hip concert. In fact, as I knew she would, she loved the whole vacation, despite no Kim Mitchell concert. He really should try harder!

I was still searching for Mitchell's solo debut EP on CD but, of course, as it didn't exist, I had no joy. Instead, I picked up the 'Best of Max Webster', which at least had 'Kids in Action' on it. It's a great collection, and probably a good starting point for budding Max newcomers.

I was getting desperate for new material from him and I was well aware that I had just made two trips to Canada without getting to a Mitchell live event. On the return flight to

England, as Ann slept beside me, I was already planning a return trip.

Canada was definitely 'stickin' my heart'!

talkers

Things were moving along quite nicely in all aspects of my life. 'Electricgarden' were working on tracks for a proposed second album. We had three or four tracks we were extremely pleased with. We also landed a plum gig as support on a festival bill, alongside '70s glamsters 'Sweet' and the 'Bay City Rollers'. As I said, things were going well.

Ann and I had an invite to a friend's 40th birthday party coming up. He was in a band and they were planning to make their first public appearance at the party. It was likely that many old friends of mine may be there, which made it a great opportunity to get reacquainted and hear what everyone had been up to over time. One 'old' friend I bumped into at the party was Mick Wilson, the drummer from the band Oxym, that I sung in around four hundred years ago! In fact, the whole band was there. It felt kind of weird!

It was really good to see Mick again. We spent a lot of the night reminiscing and laughing at all the old rockers who were still trying to 'do it'. We didn't laugh too loudly though. Disappointingly, I found out during the evening that a few months earlier, at Mick's own fortieth birthday bash, Oxym had reformed to play a short set. They had tried to contact me, but had been unable to do so. Oh well! I guess some things aren't meant to be. As we discovered we didn't live that far apart, we promised to keep in touch. It would prove to be an auspicious meeting.

Although we had worked together in a band, Mick and I hadn't really got to know each other that well. This time around, we made up for that. As time went on it transpired that we actually had a surprising amount in common. As well as being musicians and record collectors, it turned out that we were both supporters of Manchester City Football Club, in fact, we now have season tickets next to each other. We also had a liking for the same kind of bands, some of them quirky and of unusual taste. Bands like Sparks, The Tubes and more recently, Porcupine Tree. Much more importantly, I found out that Mick was a Kim Mitchell and Max Webster fan! He had been a Max fan long before I had even heard of the band. This made Mick, the first person outside of Canada, I had come across who had even heard of the band. As he relayed tales of seeing Max perform 'Paradise Skies' on Top of The Pops back in 1979, I was envious, but aware, that I had stumbled upon a truly kindred spirit.

A few months later, it became apparent to me that Electricgarden's musical direction seemed to be changing. As we began to leave the '80s feel of the band further and further behind it was replaced with more contemporary chart material, which I felt was inferior. I put up with it for a while but eventually, it wasn't to my liking and I told them I was going to leave. Unfortunately, this left the promising second album unfinished. Strangely, as soon as I had given my notice to Electricgarden, there was immediately an opportunity to join another band. It was my friend's band that I recently saw perform at his fortieth. Playing classic rock covers, we became known as 'Hair of The Dog' and after one or two further line-up changes, it became almost a 'Tokyo' reunion as Andy 'Wilko' Wilkinson joined us on guitar.

During one of our many discussions on the merits of Kim Mitchell and Max Webster, Mick and I touched on the fact of how it was criminal that not nearly enough people in England appreciated, or were even aware of this amazing legacy and talent. Casually, and without realising the consequences and repercussions of what was about to be said, we said we should form a tribute band. Once it was said, I remember there being a moment of silence as we looked at each other, allowing the words and their meaning to just hang there in the air. Could we really do this? Could we really form a Max Webster/Kim Mitchell tribute band? Would we do it, or were we just a couple of talkers?

Now... we were a drummer and a singer. That was it! Not only that, but we didn't know anyone else who had the slightest inclination of who Kim Mitchell was. Faced with this minor obstacle, how on earth were we going to find musicians who were not only good enough, but also willing to dedicate themselves to a tribute band of an artist they didn't know? In a moment of realisation, I remembered how I was always willing to rock the boat for a taste of adventure.

Despite the obvious obstacles and the odds stacked severely against us, we decided to give it a go. As brothers, bonded together and dedicated to one cause, we were now 'in search of Kim Mitchells'. Plural!

Or, on the 'look out', you might say!

what can we do with the urge

Once we had decided that we were going to create a Mitchell tribute act, we started to wonder in which direction to take. Should we concentrate on Kim Mitchell, Max Webster or both? Which musicians to ask and ultimately, who we would choose?

First off, we knew we would have to make inspired choices. Not only would they have to be excellent musicians, they would also need to have faith that Mick and I knew what we were doing. At first, rather than advertise, we decided to try the easy route and approach musicians we knew. Our first choices listened to and gave positive feedback on the music. (In hindsight, how could they not like it?). Unfortunately, as we feared, most were not willing to dedicate the time and effort that would be needed to deliver the project. Fair enough. We respected their honesty!

One of our early choices, my old friend Andy Wilkinson, who was already familiar with Kim Mitchell, said yes! perhaps as a favour to me, I think. Nevertheless, he was in and we were now a three piece. We felt at the time that Wilko would be good enough to manage all the guitar parts himself, so we were now looking for only a bass player to complete the quartet.

'Hair of The Dog' were continuing to perform during the evolution of the tribute band so, for convenience, we approached the bass player Neil, and he agreed. Done! We had the four musicians needed. We also already had rehearsal space sorted out. We were now ready to rock!

This was always going to be mine and Mick's project so it was down to us to decide what era we were going to cover. Max Webster or Kim Mitchell. After much deliberation, and to the slight disappointment of Wilko, we decided to be a Max Webster tribute.

A number of names were bandied around. One of the favourites for a while was 'Mick's Webster', but in the end, there was only ever one name, so 'The Universal Juveniles' were born.

The songs we worked on at first were what we thought would be the easiest to accomplish. We chose 'Blue River Liquor Shine', 'Check', 'Paradise Skies' and 'Coming Off the Moon'. It was slow going at first but, after a couple of weeks, we were starting to make significant progress. Some sections within the songs were really starting to sound powerful and dynamic so we were encouraged. We can do this! Early on, it was evident that for a live band without keyboards, Wilko would struggle playing all the parts that would be necessary for a full sound. We agreed to continue as a four piece until we had more material under our belts, then we would search for a second guitarist. Things were going well, and all of us seemed to be enjoying the experience.

At short notice, I felt the urge to visit Canada, and what do you do with the urge? Due to work commitments, Ann couldn't go, so it looked as though I would be on my own again, until Mick surprised me and said his lovely wife Alison was happy for us to go together. Wow! A lad's holiday, two Kim Mitchell nuts. What could possibly go wrong?

We spoke too soon. Sadly, during the time of our trip, there were no Kim Mitchell concerts scheduled in, or around, Ontario. It was late in the summer season and Mitchell had just one or two shows left to do, both of them miles away. Rather than cancel the holiday because we weren't going to be able to see Kim Mitchell perform, we decided we should try and take in visits to places associated with Kim. One prime option was to try and visit the Alert Music offices, the home of Kim Mitchell recording artist since 1982. If the mountain won't come to Mohammed and all that. Armed with the offices address and one or two other concert ideas, we set off, once more, for the Great White North.

The trip was great fun. It was Mick's first visit so we did Niagara, which is always a treat. The CN tower, Montreal, and of course, Toronto. We also visited the Sky Dome but, unfortunately, not for the Argos. Mick persuaded me to go and see The Blue Jays! The last time I went to a baseball game was back in 1986, I hadn't had the desire to go to a game since and, as we got towards the sixth inning, I understood why. Excuse me while I yawn here. Mick, being a cricket fan, loved it though and, as it was a $2 Tuesday, I didn't feel too hard done by.

We also managed to get in a couple of concerts as well. 'Trooper', who I didn't know too much about, were great fun. It was at a small, intimate club gig and they were excellent. Another night we travelled to London, Ontario to see the Australian superstars 'Powderfinger', who were promoting their 'Vulture Street' album. They were phenomenal! A superb band. Unfortunately, band wise, that was it for the holiday. All that was left for us to do was our unannounced visit to the Alert Music offices. Talk about being an anorak!

Alert Music offices were situated in a small, unassuming office block in the Moss Park area of downtown Toronto. I don't know what you should expect to encounter when you visit places like Alert, but it's rarely what you envisioned.

This was hallowed ground, the home of Kim Mitchell. I was expecting a golden halo hovering above the building, with the sound of a choir floating through the air, almost like the emerald city in the Wizard of Oz. Of course, it was nothing of the kind. A small plaque with 'Alert Music' etched on it, was all we got. But it was enough! We had arrived. Tentatively, we rang the bell.

A female voice spoke to us through the intercom. After we explained who we were and the purpose of our visit, and that we weren't international terrorist stalkers, we were buzzed into the building. We climbed a couple of flights of stairs and moved along a dimly lit corridor until we stood before a door carrying the same Alert Music plaque as we had seen downstairs. We knocked gently and, after a couple of seconds, the door was opened by Tom Berry, President of Alert, former managing director of Anthem Records and Kim Mitchell's manager since the early 1980's. Shaking our hands, he beckoned us inside where we were introduced to the beautiful Jesse Kline, who is head of relations at the company.

The office was small, with walls adorned with photographs of familiar faces. I recognised Holly Cole and of course, Kim Mitchell. Also in the room was the real wall of fame! I was astounded to see gold and platinum albums for 'Akimbo Alogo', 'Shaking Like a Human Being', 'Rockland', 'I Am a Wild Party (Live)', 'Aural Fixations', 'Itch' and 'Greatest Hits'. This was definitely the inner sanctum, the centre of operations for Canada's greatest musician. We were in our element and felt humbled in the presence of such achievements.

The team of Tom and Jesse seemed small for such a major organisation, but I suppose that, if you know what you are doing and are good at your work as these two obviously were, then how many staff members do you really need?

Tom and Jesse were gracious with their time and were terrific, if somewhat bemused hosts. They answered all our questions, unfortunately not always to our liking. No, Kim didn't have a new album in the pipeline and he didn't have any concerts scheduled in the near future. In fact, he wasn't even in town. It transpired that he owned a cottage somewhere in northern Ontario and spent most of his time there. He hardly ever called into the office and to be honest, they hadn't seen him for a few weeks now. Oh well! We hadn't expected to meet him anyway. To be welcomed into and to be able to stand within the office was prize enough.

They told us a little about Alert, which, Tom informed us, had been founded by himself as a music publishing and managing company in 1984 and later became an actual record label as well. It was all fascinating and we would have loved to have stayed longer but they were obviously busy, and we were probably stopping them from completing their daily business. We thanked them for their time and turned to leave.

Before we could go, Tom told us to hang on a moment as he might have something in the back for us. He disappeared into another room, leaving us hoping that he would return with Kim Mitchell, a little dusty and confused having been misplaced a few weeks earlier. Instead, he returned with an armful of posters advertising Kim Mitchell tours and albums. It was all excellent material and would eventually go to cover the 'Universal Juveniles" rehearsal room, providing memories and inspiration whenever it was needed.

The afternoon had been amazing. We couldn't thank them enough for their time and generosity. After saying our goodbyes, we turned to leave. As we approached the door, it opened itself and... in walked Kim Mitchell!

No, this isn't some sort of wind up or a case of mistaken identity, it was truly the great man himself. Think about this scenario for a moment. What are the chances of travelling 3,500 miles and without prior planning, bumping into the one person you hoped to see? Unbelievable! We were speechless!

Kim seemed a little taken aback by encountering two strangers in the office. At first there was just silence between us, as Kim looked at both Mick and I and we glanced at each other. Neither party could speak. Eventually, Tom broke the awkward silence and introduced us. Once it had been explained to him who we were and why we were there, you could see Kim physically relax and smile as he shook our hands. He appeared cool in shorts, T-shirt and shades and looked extremely healthy. We told him how much his music had meant to us over the years and informed him that we were in a Max Webster tribute band back home in England. What he said in response to that will live with me for ever more. His simple retort to the information that we were in a Max Webster tribute act was... "Why?"

Mick and I nearly fell on the floor with laughter. What a perfect response. He was obviously confused as to why anyone would want to waste their time playing Max songs. When we asked him what he himself was up to he stated that he "had a whole bunch of songs written" but that he didn't know what he was going to do with them. He continued by saying that "No-one likes our fucking music anymore!"

In hindsight, knowing what Kim had had to go through to see the release of 'Kimosabe' and the Canadian music industry's disgusting apathy to that release, this bitter comment makes more sense. But, being a fan, I have to admit that it hurt a little at the time.

Both Mick and I enthused to Kim about our appreciation of his later work. Mick being very much a fan of 'Kimosabe' and I telling him that 'Itch' was a particular favourite of mine. Kim acknowledged 'Itch' as one of his favourites also.

We asked if the Kim Mitchell Band was rehearsing and he said they never rehearsed but, if they were, he would have gladly invited us down to watch. Unfortunately, he politely declined our suggestion to arrange an impromptu rehearsal, which was a bit selfish of him really, but we'll forgive him.

We managed to get some photographs taken, and he signed the posters we'd been given. One of the photographs of Kim, Mick and me was actually placed upon Kim's website for a while. That gave us a tremendous kick whenever we viewed it and it was also proof that the meeting had even taken place. Sometimes I had to pinch myself to be sure that it ever happened. It had been an unbelievable afternoon. We thanked him, Tom and Jesse for their time and floated downstairs, as if in a dream. What a wonderful experience. After many years, I had finally met my hero. First contact! Hopefully, the first of many.

Just before we returned home to England, we called back at the Alert building and presented gifts of flowers for the office and a Manchester City Football Club shirt for Kim, who sadly wasn't there this time. They were surprised and pleased with the gifts, although I've never seen any photographs of Kim wearing the shirt. Never mind, we hope it made him smile.

It had been a fantastic holiday, one that will live with me for a long time to come. The meeting with Kim had been inspirational and I now had an uncontrollable urge to get the 'Universal Juveniles' up and running properly. Nothing could stop us now. Could it?

Oh yes it could. Life is always ready to throw a few surprises at you, particularly when you think things are going smoothly. Apparently, at home, there had been some unrest within the 'Hair of The Dog' ranks while I had been away. This, as luck would have it, would have a profound effect upon the current state and progress of The Universal Juveniles.

One step forward, two steps back! The 'dreamthieves' were in town!

lager and ann

While I had been away, it appeared that a disagreement had developed between the drummer and some other members of 'Hair of The Dog' including me, which seemed strange seeing as how I had been 3,500 miles away at the time. We struggled to find any resolution to the situation and were unable to reassure the drummer or help him with his issues. In the end, we had to let him go.

As we had a number of engagements that we needed to honour, Mick, reluctantly at first, agreed to join us. This was good news all around for the band. Mick was a much better drummer and it meant that 'Hair of The Dog' came on leaps and bounds, (no pun intended) in a short space of time. On the down side, it also meant that, due to rehearsal and gigging commitments, there was no way that we could continue with 'The Universal Juveniles'. Not for the time being anyway.

We put the Juveniles on hold, not realising at the time that it would be an incredible two and a half years before we had the time to resurrect the project. No Kim Mitchell activity? I was worried that I may start to suffer withdrawal symptoms if I wasn't careful. A saviour appeared though, to soften the blow. Kim Mitchell's debut EP had finally been released on CD courtesy of Wounded Bird Records. The reproduction is exceptional, from the cover to the sound. It had been a long time coming, but well worth the wait. This meant that I had now managed to collect all Max and Kim's albums on CD. All we needed now was a new album from Kim. I hoped we wouldn't have to wait too long.

Mick fell into the swing of things with the band and we were soon back on the road. Unfortunately, we lost our bass player Neil. Due to family commitments he had to leave the band and we had to find a replacement. It turned out, it also meant we had lost him from 'The Universal Juveniles' too, but we wouldn't realise that for quite some time. Mick's joining the band also meant that it was easier to suggest doing a Kim Mitchell song to the rest of the guys. We eventually settled on 'Go for Soda', as we felt its commerciality would most easily appeal to the English punters.

We rocked our version up a little more than Kim's, trying to keep it within the same vein as our other material. It was 'riffier' and rougher around the edges. The audience response to it was quite remarkable. It really started off going down well, which bode well for the future, and the time that the Juveniles would eventually reunite.

Everything else in my life was pretty good at the time. Work continued to be rewarding, the band was good and my daughter, Leigh-Anne, was growing up into a beautiful young lady; although she could still be quite a handful at times! I was also... Shock! Horror!... head over heels in love. Ann was everything I had ever wanted and was easily the best thing that had happened to me since the birth of Leigh-Anne. She even indulged me in my obsession with Mr Mitchell. I would be a fool to myself if I were to let Ann slip through my fingers. There was only one thing for it. I decided that I was going to ask Ann to marry me!

I wanted to do it with some style and panache. After all, she deserved it. After much thought, I knew there was only one place on earth suitable for my proposal, I wanted us to be on a boat, on Lake Ontario, overlooking Toronto's skyline at sunset! Romantic or what?

I contacted Rick and told him my plans. After chiding me that she deserved better, he told me not to worry and to leave everything with him and he would sort out all the arrangements at his end. I managed to get Ann's ring size and secreted a ring into my luggage. So far so good. All I had to do was keep everything a secret from Ann. Easier said than done.

With only a couple of weeks to go before our time in Canada, Ann hit me with a suggestion that she had been toying with for a while. Instead of spending most of our time in the Kitchener area, not the most romantic of areas, why didn't we hire a cottage in the north for part of the stay? Ordinarily, I would have agreed that this was a marvellous suggestion but, as I didn't know the exact details of Rick's plans for the big night yet, I was unable to agree to the cottage idea. I explained that our Canadian friends, knowing we were coming, may have made plans. Why not wait until we arrived and see what transpired? Now, Ann isn't someone you can manipulate very easily. Quite rightly, she believed the cottage to be a wonderful idea and was sure that our friends would understand. I needed another plan of attack! Quickly! I went on to explain that the holiday had already cost quite a bit of money and that I wasn't sure if I could afford a cottage as well. She was nothing if not persistent. "Why? What have you spent all your money on?" Maybe I should have come clean at this point but being a man, I had another idea. I replied by saying...

"What I spend my money on is my business!"

I know! I know! A brilliant response! She accused me of purely wanting to go to Canada for myself, not caring if she were there or not. She went on to say that if that were the case, then I could go on my own. She was no longer coming!

Superb! Two weeks to go until the trip. All the meticulous planning in place. An engagement ring purchased and my fiancé had dumped me! How could she think that I was only thinking of myself regarding the holiday? Ok, I know she was unaware of my engagement plans, but... Come on! In hindsight, it's a good job that she didn't know I had already made plans to see Kim Mitchell in a town called Strathroy whilst we were there. I think that might have been the straw that broke the camel's back if she knew.

Dumbfounded, I had to think on my feet. I did the only thing I could think of to do. I made her feel bad about herself! I told her that, as it was to be her birthday while we were in Canada, our friends and I had planned a surprise evening for her, but that she had now spoiled it for herself and everyone else. Boy! I feel bad about myself as I think back to this incident.

Ann was mortified and after a few days, she began to speak to me again. Ann is never the quickest person to make an apology. I told her that the plans were still in place and that she would have to pretend to be surprised on the night. May God strike me down! The trip was back on.

...Fast forward...

When we arrived at Rick's I managed to slip the engagement ring to him for safe keeping and to stop Ann coming across it by accident. He told me that he had booked a boat trip from the Toronto harbour on the last Saturday evening of our stay. The evening included a dinner dance during the three-hour cruise and was due to return to the harbour after sundown. It seemed like everything I had hoped for. He also completely shocked me by stating that a hoard of people I knew were going to be there as they all wanted to share the occasion with us. All in all, around thirteen friends would be there. I was overwhelmed. I only hoped that everything would go according to plan.

We had a wonderful time during the first few days, visiting friends and sightseeing. We even canoed (or is it kayaked? I can never seem to get that right!) along the Grand River. A wonderful experience, even though the only wildlife we saw were herons. We also managed to see Colin James at the same venue as I had seen Trooper some time ago. He was fantastic. Incredibly energetic and worked the crowd really well.

I was aware, by this time, that Kim Mitchell had started broadcasting as a DJ for Q107, and worked out of the Hard Rock Cafe in Toronto. This meant that I knew exactly where he would be and at what time. What right minded, fanatical stalker could resist? We arrived at the Hard Rock around thirty minutes before Kim was due to start. I was browsing in the shop when, out of the corner of my eye, I caught sight of his familiar figure slip quietly into the broadcasting booth.

My God! He was here! I couldn't believe it. All of a sudden, I came over all anxious and was unable to approach him. I was a bag of nerves; I needed a drink! Deciding that Kim, as well as myself, needed time to settle in, we went to the bar where I quickly downed two pints of lager. Ann suggested that we order some food while I prepared myself. After two pints of lager, this seemed a good idea. Whilst waiting for the waiter, I downed another quick lager.

The waiter came over with menus and recommended the days' special, Tuna. I hardly ever eat fish, and would never dream of ordering it in a restaurant. To be honest, I was more concerned with the fact that I was in the same building as Kim Mitchell than ordering food, not only that but he was only a few feet away behind a glass wall. I kept muttering to myself "That's Kim Mitchell!"

I ordered some more drinks and said OK to the Tuna. When I was asked how I would like the Tuna prepared, I didn't really care or have a clue. Not meaning to be rude, I pointed at something on the menu. "You do realise that is raw, sir?" asked the waiter. Whilst looking at Kim I simply nodded, and the waiter walked off.

Just as I had decided I would nip along Yonge Street and try to buy a couple of CDs for Kim to sign, the drinks arrived. Not to be put off by this, I quickly downed my fourth pint and dashed out to the record store. Suitably refreshed from city centre air, I returned just as the food arrived. I ordered more drinks and took a bite of the tuna. "It's fucking raw!" I cried, pulling the fish from my mouth. Ann just rolled her eyes at me.

I tried my best, but I just couldn't eat it. When the waiter returned with our drinks, I asked him if he could go and cook the fish for me. As he took the tuna back to the kitchen, he looked at me like I was a complete moron! Rightly so, I suppose.

After the food, which was delicious, and another pint, I felt it was time to meet my old friend and hero. The lager I had consumed had given me the courage I needed to approach Kim and had also steadied my nerves considerably. The only trouble was, I had never been a good afternoon drinker. The lagers had gone straight to my head. As I tapped gently upon the broadcasting booth, Kim quietly, opened the door and slipped outside. Trying to introduce myself, and to my absolute horror, I found that I could hardly speak. My mouth moved, but I was making no sense whatsoever. The combination of nerves, awe and lager had rendered me an imbecile! If the waiter had seen me, it would have confirmed the impression he already had of me.

Ann took over the conversation while I collected myself, and saved the day. Eventually, I was able to join in. Incredibly, Kim remembered me even asking how the band was doing, although he was still a little confused about the idea of a Max tribute existing in England. He seemed genuinely pleased to see us although, between you and me, I think he was more pleased to see Ann, who is a bit of a stunner! I asked how the new record was going and he surprised me by saying it was already out! This confused me, as I had no idea what he was talking about. Touche!

I went on to tell him that we were going to be seeing him perform in Strathroy in a few days and he told me to leave our names with him and he would put us on the guest list. Unbelievable! I nearly fell through the floor. I was going to be a guest of Kim Mitchell's. It was more than I could have hoped for.

He signed the CDs I had brought and he wished us well, adding that he looked forward to seeing us at the show. Shaking our hands, we said our farewells.

Amazing! What an encounter. I was in heaven. Drunk, but in heaven. As we left the restaurant that day, Ann by my side and a future guest of, none other than, Kim Mitchell, I felt like the most important person in the world. I was bursting at the seams with pride. 'I walk tall, never fearing the edge.'

~~~~~~~~~~~~~~~~~~~~~

You know how there are often two or more sides to a story? Well, we will never know how, or if, Kim would remember this encounter with a drunk fan from the UK. But I know someone who was there and can recall what happened in great detail. Ann was only too delighted to recall the meeting and my behaviour in excruciating detail. I can't read it...

Ann's recollections:

"I remember that Kim Mitchell (whom I wouldn't know from Adam) was doing his radio show from inside, what can best be described as a 'glass booth', so he was clearly visible. Unfortunately, he was clearly visible to Pete as well. To this day I pray it was some kind of two-way glass and Kim Mitchell couldn't see this weird, nervous, lunatic loitering outside.

Next to the 'booth', there was a small Hard Rock Cafe boutique selling T-shirts etc. Pete was hanging around this store for ages, pretending to peruse the merchandise, but it was clear to anyone that all he was doing was 'ogling' his hero through the glass.

Back and forth. Back and forth. Much to the annoyance of the staff who asked him a number of times if they could help him. He clearly appeared furtive and suspicious They were obviously beginning to think he was a shoplifter. I had never seen him acting like this. He was literally regressing before my eyes.

Eventually, he found the courage to gently 'tap' on the glass and got Kim's attention, if he hadn't already. Just as I thought that this behavioural madness was over, on Kim's emergence from the booth, things quickly deteriorated even further. Pete lost the power of speech.

Kim Mitchell appeared impossibly tall. I believe he's 6' something. I'm only 5'1" and here I was, craning my neck upward and, almost, holding the hand of a 'gibbering' chimpanzee. I could see that Kim was quickly becoming a little confused and even unsettled by the situation. I cut into the conversation, if you could call it that, and introduced Pete to Kim. I remember he smiled, obviously believing I was Pete's carer!

Pete eventually calmed down and he and Kim had a short conversation. Kim seemed to remember Pete from a previous encounter. He then invited us as his guests to a concert that we were going to in a few days. We said our goodbyes and Kim 'gratefully' slipped back into the booth.

I can smile now at the memory of this incident, but that's only with the knowledge that I'll never have to go through it again.

…Weird!"

got lucky (boat/ & girl/)

When we returned to Rick's in Cambridge, I immediately telephoned Mick in England. I wanted to tell him all about the encounter with Kim Mitchell and the guest list incident, but I also wanted to discuss Kim's confusing statement that his new album was "already out!" Mick told me to leave it with him and when and if he found anything out, he would call me back at Rick's. Comfortable that the dilemma was in the capable hands of my 'partner in crime', I settled into the continuation of the holiday.

Next on the agenda was the Kim Mitchell Band in concert in Strathroy, Ontario. Four of us made the journey; Rick, Jimmy, Ann and I. The show was to be an outdoor festival and headlined by Sass Jordan, a female rocker whom I didn't know too much about, other than Rick quite liked her.

When we arrived at the gate, sure enough, there we were on the guest list! Our names were in huge, neon lights next to that of Kim Mitchell's. Ok... they were on an A4 piece of paper in black ink. I managed to procure the guest list later on, and yes, I've still got it!

The show was totally fantastic. The sun was blazing hot, the crowd were rocking, the beer was flowing and I danced like a lunatic all the way through Kim's set. The set wasn't too different from the first time I had seen him. Full of crowd favourites, but nothing from later albums such as 'Kimosabe', which was a shame. He did perform a new song though, an unaccompanied version of 'Killer's Name' from the yet to be released 'Ain't Life Amazing' album. He also finished the show by segueing into the instrumental, fade-out section of Max Webster's 'Beyond the Moon', which was awesome! What a show! I was blown away!

After his set, Kim was at the side of the stage with other fans milling round him. It was all very relaxed so we managed to get his attention briefly and tell him how much we enjoyed the show. He seemed pleased with how it went and was quite happy to spend a few minutes with us. I'm sure he remembered us from the Hard Rock Café as it was only a few days ago but I was glad I was more 'together' for this meeting. I managed to get a couple of good photographs of Kim, Ann and myself. We thanked him and made our way back to the front of the stage. We stayed for a couple of Sass Jordan numbers, and she seemed quite good but, it was a long drive and the designated driver wanted to get back. A wonderful, wonderful day!

During the journey home, we blasted out Kim Mitchell songs through the car stereo. Reliving the concert and loud enough to wake the dead. With Ann asleep beside me, I rode home on a wave of euphoria. A stupid grin plastered on my face. Boy! I loved this country. What a day!

A few days later, and true to his word, Mick telephoned back with the news that Kim Mitchell's new album was indeed out! With growing excitement, I listened as Mick went on to tell me that it was called 'Fill Your Head with Rock' and was a compilation album. I suddenly felt deflated. Disappointed! Six years since the release of 'Kimosabe' and still no new material? He went on to say that it did include a new track, the 'Fill Your Head with Rock' title track. So, not all bad news then. He also informed me that it was a two-disc set and included a DVD of a live concert recorded on the 'Rockland' tour. What? I was stunned. At last. A live DVD. Mick hadn't finished though. The information got better and better. He went on to say that, if we ordered it from a certain retailer, the delivery would include a free Fill Your Head with Rock' T-shirt.

Overjoyed, I asked Mick if he would kindly order it for me and I would settle up with him when I got home. Typically, it seemed that Mick had been toying with me all along. Not only had he already placed the order but it had also already arrived and was waiting for me. I almost wanted to cut the holiday short and go home there and then, so that I could put on my free T-shirt and rock out to the video.

Of course, that would not be possible. Kim, for once, would have to come second. I had the big night to think about. The moment of truth. Would she say yes? Could I be that lucky? Or, and not for the first time on this holiday, would I be left looking like an utter rejected moron? Saturday night around sunset, I would know the answer. For the next few nights, I could hardly sleep at all.

On the evening of the boat trip, Toronto's weather was, predictably, gorgeous. The sun had been beating down all day. When we arrived for the launch, I was overwhelmed that everyone who had expressed a desire to be with us was there. I was really touched by their presence. Of course, Ann was also delighted, but believed it was all in aid of her birthday.

As we set sail, I asked Rick, not for the first or last time that evening, whether he had the ring with him. He reassured me everything was in order and not to worry. To help calm me down, he brought over some drinks for us. In fact, drinks were coming fast and furious from all directions. I was drinking red wine and, by around nine thirty, must have had at least two bottles worth to myself. Ordinarily, I would have been very drunk on that much wine, but my nerves and anxiety were both assisting in keeping me sober. Or so I believed!

As the evening wore on and the sun over Toronto began to set, I was aware that the evening was getting later and that the time was drawing near. Just one more quick drink, Dutch courage, and all that, and one last visit to the washroom and I would be ready. I had put it off long enough.

As I headed toward the washroom, I passed by Jimmy, who gave me such a withering stare of exasperation, as he looked between me and his watch, that I knew the time had to be now. Diverting from the washroom, I made my way directly toward Ann and asked her if she would like to join me on deck, to watch the sunset? With a lovely warm smile, she politely... declined!

What? That wasn't the plan! She went on to say that it was cold on deck, she hadn't realised that boats could be so cold and she didn't have a coat. Quick! Quick! Somebody must have a coat we could borrow. I managed to blag a fleece off somebody, presented it to Ann, and asked her again. This time, she reluctantly agreed, stating that it obviously meant so much to me.

All our friends had already made their way on deck as we made our way to the boat side to view the skyline. Ann was correct, it was surprisingly chilly outside, but the skyline looked fantastic. This was it. Everything, against all the odds, had worked out, and it had all come down to this one moment. We were on Lake Ontario. There was the Toronto skyline. Here was Ann, looking wonderful, if a little strange in a borrowed oversized fleece. And it was sunset. There could be no more delays or excuses.

Leaning in toward Ann, I asked her if she had had a nice evening. I took her silence to be a yes, and continued, telling her that the evening hadn't really been for her birthday after all. She looked at me, still didn't say anything, smiled, then turned away from me to look toward the harbour.

What was wrong with her? Why wasn't she speaking? Then, it dawned on me. I was having another Hard Rock Cafe moment. I wasn't sober at all. How could I be after two and a half bottles of red? I was speaking, but making no sense at all. The Hard Rock waiter would have loved this!

Trying to collect myself, I leaned into Ann and tried again. I got half way through the "Tonight wasn't really for your birthday" speech, when Ann turned to me and snapped "What are you on about?"

Wide eyed, I blurted out... "Will you marry me?"

Ann continued to stare at me for a second or two longer then, suddenly, she threw her hands to her face in shock! Then her arms were thrust around my neck and she started sobbing uncontrollably. "Is that a yes?" I laughed. All she could do was nod her wet face into my shoulder. Honestly! Girls!

I turned towards our friends, who were waiting patiently in the cool breeze. I offered them a thumbs up and an almighty cheer erupted on deck. Rick handed me the ring, which fit perfectly, and that was it. Success! A wonderful feeling. Ann had agreed to be my wife. I was ecstatic! The happiest man on earth! Especially when Ann realised what all the secrecy and fuss had been about that cottage business. After she realised what she had put me through, she grovelled for weeks. Ok! Days... Alright... Hours! This is Ann we're talking about, after all.

Well, what can I say? Canada really does it for me. I know I've said it before but what a superb vacation. Easily my greatest ever holiday.

My very own 'big best summer'. Wonderful!

cry out your wife

'Fill Your Head with Rock' turned out to be an excellent compilation. In contrast to the Greatest Hits album, it leaned more towards the rockier side of Kim and tried not to duplicate that album's track listing as much as possible. It concentrated more on tracks from the later albums, like 'Aural Fixations', 'Itch' and 'Kimosabe', although 'Go for Soda', 'Lager & Ale' etc. were inevitable but welcome inclusions.

The 'Fill Your Head with Rock' track itself is easily the heaviest thing Kim Mitchell has recorded in years, possibly since his debut EP in 1982. Produced by Joe Hardy, who also plays bass, the Kim Mitchell Band, for this song, is a stripped-down affair and features Greg Morrow on drums and Pete Fredette on backing vocals.

Beginning with wildly distorted bass and guitars and accompanied by heavy, pounding drums from Morrow, the song explodes from the speakers, before Mitchell begins to spit and snarl his vocals with venom. The song rocks and is a shocking reminder of what a great band this is. The vibe is powerful, but is over all too soon and leaves you looking forward to an album of all new material from the obviously rejuvenated Kim Mitchell.

The song is a collaboration between Mitchell and Craig Baxter. Baxter is a friend of Kim's, who placed postings on Mitchell's web-site. Kim enjoyed the prose of the postings and approached Baxter as a potential collaborator. The stuff of dreams for Craig, I'm sure, but it seems to work. An interesting story and an interesting song.

The real meat of this package, though, is the DVD. Recorded at The Kee to Bala, Ontario, on the 'Rockland' tour of 1989, it is simply stunning. The band is on fire, the song selection is bang on and the sound and camera work are tremendous. It only makes you wonder why it took an amazing sixteen years to be commercially released. I guess we'll never know why it wasn't released earlier.

Superb though! At long last, a Kim Mitchell DVD concert. Long overdue. All we had to do now was wait for a new album and, if the 'Fill Your Head with Rock' track was any indication, the prospect looked intriguingly promising!

'Hair of The Dog' continued to move from strength to strength. Over time, we had become a really tight professional little outfit and a force to be reckoned with on the local scene. Whenever we played, the venues were usually packed to the rafters and rocking! Unfortunately, the narrow mindedness of the punters had resulted in the band having to drop 'Go for Soda' from the set. Despite being presented with songs to make them think, they would cry out, continuously, for familiar numbers. We had to settle for playing songs that were really well known, or risk the chance of the work drying up! I was beginning to feel that my time of singing for the public was nearing its end.

As plans for the wedding approached, I was astounded to hear that five of our Canadian brethren were planning to make the trip out to be with us. We were so pleased that they would be there, not only because of the wedding, but it would also give us a chance to return a small part of the generosity and hospitality that had been shown to myself and Ann over the years.

All five; Rick and his lovely girlfriend Gail, Jimmy and his wonderful wife Val and our good friend David 'Mitch' Mitchell (no relation) would all be staying with us at our home. Our home is your home, as they say. It would be cramped but fun.

I arranged for the band to play twice when the Canadians arrived, once at a local bar, and also at the wedding's evening reception. I didn't realise it at the time, but these would be two of the last shows that 'Hair of The Dog' would ever perform.

The wedding went without incident and it was a wonderful occasion, even if I do say so myself. Ann looked stunning that day and when I saw her walk down the aisle, I fell in love with her all over again. I felt so privileged that she had agreed to be my wife. I'm also pleased to say that the band performed superbly at both shows. Could life be any better?

A romantic footnote to this episode is that, before flying home, Rick and Gail got engaged to be married on the Isle of Mull in Scotland. When romance is in the air, it's in the air!

After the wedding and when the Canadians had returned home, 'Hair of The Dog' performed one more show after which, our bass player Craig, snapped a tendon in his hand, presumably whilst he was tying his shoe lace. Don't even go there! We had to give him time to heal, so we cancelled a few shows. Then a few more, Then a few more! Before we knew it, the band had simply slipped away. Peacefully.

No one had seemed particularly interested in finding a replacement for Craig, even though we had even discussed playing a few dates in Canada. A few people I knew all owned bars in Ontario and Quebec and were interested in putting us on. We worked out the logistics and found it was feasible. Of course, this never happened, and we put the band to bed.

With myself, Mick and Wilko all out of work musically there seemed only one logical thing to do. After two and a half years in the wilderness, it was time to put 'The Universal Juveniles' back into action.

Twenty-five years of throwing 'pearls before swine' were officially over. It was time for some 'Diamonds, Diamonds'!

juveniles won't stop

Discovering 'Ain't Life Amazing' (2007)

As 'The Universal Juveniles' finally shook off the cobwebs and reconvened, we had already decided that a second guitarist was going to be essential to accompany Wilko. We also knew that the project was probably going to be a studio only affair, not a live proposition as previously intended. Everybody seemed cool with the idea.

We approached our old bass player Neil to re-join, only to find out he had decided to hang up his bass for good. We now needed a bass player as well as a second guitarist.

A few of the possible choices for a second guitarist all passed, stating that the material would take too long to master and they were unwilling to commit to such a long project. We appreciated the honesty. Luckily, the prime candidate we were after fell in love with the Max material and signed on. Welcome on-board Baz Oldale! Baz is an exceptional guitarist whose reputation locally, is formidable. It was an honour to have him on board.

Bass guitar wise, we struggled for quite a while, until someone suggested a nineteen-year-old local lad who would be more than capable. We approached Nathan Gibbons with the material and, after listening to it for a few days, he told us he was willing to give it a go. Due to his age, we didn't fully commit to Nathan being in the band straight away, but after only the first rehearsal he had displayed that his ability and commitment to learning the songs was incredibly professional for one so young. Within an hour, he was in. We now had 'The Universal Juveniles'. Mark two, complete!

During the extended layoff, Mick and I had never stopped working on the potential song choices for the project. Despite this, by the time we began the second phase, we had only agreed on around half of the songs; 'Coming Off the Moon', 'Blue River Liquor Shine', 'Check', 'Words to Words' and 'Distressed'. Unusual choices perhaps, but we were determined to make these songs work.

Rehearsals began with the understanding that we would introduce the other five songs as we progressed. Once more, we started off a little patchy, but after a few weeks real progress was being made and we were able to introduce 'April in Toledo' into our list of songs.

After finally dragging myself into the twentieth century and obtaining a computer, I had been aware of the recent release of Kim's 'Ain't Life Amazing' album and managed to get myself a copy. The internet had completely changed the record buyer's world. Retail outlets had all but disappeared and hunting now took place online. More convenient perhaps, but a lot of the drama and mystique had now gone from the activity. Despite this, I still felt incredible joy at receiving Kim's new release. It had now been an unacceptable eight years since 'Kimosabe'. Would the wait be worth it?

For a CD, 'Ain't Life Amazing' is a stunningly well-presented release, although my love of the old-fashioned LP covers just won't go away. It's easily the best CD packaging of Mitchell's career. The liner notes are informative and the photography of the band is excellent, showing them in a light-hearted mood. As with the 'Fill Your Head with Rock' track, which appears as a hidden bonus here, the band personnel and production duties by Joe Hardy, is the same.

Opening with the storming title track and leadoff single, the album never lets up for a minute. Starting with distorted guitar and stomping drum fade-in, the song thunders into life with Mitchell's eerily contorted, venomous vocal. This is heavy stuff. Hardy's production is loud and the unusual over distortion adds an unsettling feeling. Despite this being an incredibly heavy song, the chorus is amazingly catchy and sing-a-long, helping to give Mitchell a surprise summer radio hit. Well deserved, I might add.

'Rock That Rhyme' continues in a similar style. Although slightly less intense to start with, the chorus is punchy and the whole thing rocks with an attitude not heard from Mitchell since his Max Webster days. The arrangement is played fairly straight, allowing Mitchell's superb guitar work to shine through. After only two songs, it's evident that the eight-year lay off from recording has not meant Mitchell has been idle. His guitar playing is incredible here.

'I Got a Line on You' continues the onslaught. This album is rock with a capital R! A very different Kim Mitchell Band is on the loose, and their intent is clear. This is Mitchell's heaviest album of his career. Morrow's drums and Hardy's bass provide a rock steady backbeat to Kim's wall of sound guitars. Fredette's vocal, a little less up front than usual, is nevertheless ever present and helps make the choruses extremely powerful.

After such a heavy three song attack, 'Love Overtime' is almost like light relief. Giving us a chance to take in some air. A superb song and one of the best on the album. Mitchell's vocals are phenomenal. Powerful and emotive. Starting with acoustic guitar, it soon shifts up a gear into a wonderful mid-paced, lighter-wielding rock ballad anthem. This has hit single written all over it. It's also evident that, in Craig Baxter, Kim Mitchell may well have found the perfect replacement for Pye Dubois as the lyrics here are simply wonderful. A fantastic song!

'Bad Times' is perhaps the albums first slip in quality. It's a simplistic riff, with a bit of a mindless chorus. In a live context it probably works much better, but on record and up against the excellent standard of material on show here, you can't help but think Mitchell, and Baxter to be fair, are capable of much better.

'Dreamthieves' restores the quality in some style. An unusual and atmospheric arrangement, its dizzying complexity is simply staggering. A wonderful construction of a song. Morrow, perhaps for the first time, is able to display what he is capable of. A stunning performance all round, including Baxter's lyrical talent. It reminds me of Max Webster at their most mischievous.

Wow! Half way through and the album is already outstanding. Over the eight years, the KMB have evolved into a very different beast. Still able to shock, surprise and astound. A new Mitchell album is an event! An experience to be savoured. After listening to the first six tracks a few times, I felt suitably ready for the second half of the album.

'Space' is another mini masterpiece. With a growling rhythm and heavy percussion, the song has a groove reminiscent to 'That's The Hold' from 'Shaking Like a Human Being', but Hardy's production renders it nothing like it's distant cousin. Mitchell's vocals, distorted beyond recognition, are vicious and direct. A wonderful, atmospheric number. Extremely powerful!

'In The Stars Tonight' slows things down a little. A bluesy, swampy song with a soaring chorus. Mitchell's delicate guitar touches here are a joy and a master class in taste.

Next up is 'Killer's Name', the song I first heard a year or so earlier in Strathroy. This is a very different animal to that version though. A full band, up-beat version. Continuing the bluesy feel of 'In the Stars Tonight', it's similar in feel to 'Big Smoke' from 'Aural Fixations' but, as with every presentation on this album, it's more intense and alarming. A superb guitar solo brings the song to a disjointed, dramatic, collapsed stop! Tremendous!

'Lick A Message' is a light, fun rocker in an almost 'Van Halen' style (when they were capable of writing good songs). A great groove and with a lyric that Pye would have been proud of. A fantastic performance from all, and the jokey feel of the song, with its false ending, sets us up nicely for the excellent album closer.

'Nawlin's Nights' is simply stunning. The track features the welcome return of Ken 'Spider' Sinnaeve on bass, who last appeared on the 'Itch' album. I defy anyone to be able to keep their dancing feet still when they hear this one. Brighter and more uplifting than most of the other darker material. It's the perfect choice to close the album. A quirky arrangement with a plethora of backing vocals and voices thrown into the mix. A wonderful song which keeps you on your toes and guessing to the end. Fantastic!

What an incredible return to form. For a performer in his, dare I say it, 'twilight years', Mitchell still sounds fresh, relevant and downright exciting. Younger pretenders to the rock throne should take heed. I was breathless!

The unbelievably high quality of the album caused a slight dilemma in the Juveniles camp for a short time. We all loved the album and hinted at the prospect of including a track on our own album. Of course, that would have changed the whole dynamic of the band. In the end, we decided to stay as a Max tribute only. But... there's always a next time!

Returning to the Juveniles, the songs were progressing wonderfully, although we still had a long way to go. We had also decided that we would try to include an original number on the record. One inspired by and reminiscent of a Mitchell/Dubois composition. This meant that Mick and I had to decide on the final three songs as soon as possible.

To help us in our task, we had the idea of performing some research; of going on a fact-finding mission. That's correct, another visit to Canada was on the horizon. We convinced the wives that it would be beneficial to us and the project to return to Canada, and they fell for it! Although I'm sure they didn't really mind anyway.

The trip was on. This time, we were determined that everything would go to plan. We would have a meeting with and see Kim Mitchell in concert. And also have some, unexpected, encounters with some other relevant cast members. This time, nothing would stop us.

O' Canada, stand on guard for me! It was time to meet some 'overseas sensations'!

in a world with giants

Ahead of our visit, our friend Rick had already obtained tickets to see the Kim Mitchell Band at the Belgian Club in Delhi, Ontario. This time there would be no missing out. We would definitely be seeing the master at work, and it would be the very first time for Mick. I envied him. You always remember your first time, right?

The show was a sensation. A full Kim Mitchell indoor show! Two hours! Due to the length of the show, there were quite a few surprises for me this time, although still nothing was performed from the underrated 'Kimosabe' sct. Perhaps the album was still too painful a memory for Kim to return to.

There were a couple of songs from 'Ain't Life Amazing', but the real gems were a version of Max Webster's 'A Million Vacations' and at the end of the set, an extended instrumental coda of 'Beyond the Moon'. We were in our element and were stood right at the foot of the stage like star-struck teenagers. Wonderful! We didn't get the chance to speak with him at the show. To be honest, we didn't really try, as we knew what it was like after a show, you really just want some time to yourself.

We had a lot of plans for the trip but, with a two-week window, we thought everything should be relaxed and spaced out nicely. Think again. We ended having to cram everything into a two-day slot. Rick, who had recently bought a trailer in the north, was determined that we should experience it and had planned a trip out. Ann would have been envious of us, but we wondered if we would have the time to fit everything in.

To add to the scheduling nightmare, Mick had the crazy idea of trying to set up a meeting with his hero, Gary McCracken. Seeing Kim perform the Gary McCracken penned 'A Million Vacations' had inspired him in his quest.

Knowing we had a busy few days ahead of us, we had decided to spend an afternoon in Kitchener at our friend's home, Jim Hallam, also affectionately known as 'Jimmy the Tooth', as he was the local dentist.

Whilst I was lounging around the pool area, Mick was inside researching and browsing the Internet. All of a sudden, he appeared on the patio with a huge grin on his face. 'Oh no!' I thought, 'what now?'.

I'll let Mick tell the next part of the story:

We were sitting around the pool at Jimmy Hallam's home with a bit of time to kill. "I wonder what Garry McCracken's doing?" I said randomly to Pete, as we were in a Max Webster frame of mind and had been googling various Max Webster people - Pye Dubois, Dave Myles, Mike Tilka, Paul Kearsey, Terry Watkinson etc.

I googled Gary on my phone and came across an advert from a music store website which showed he gave drum lessons. I called the store, and was told that Gary no longer worked from the store but still gave lessons from his home. He gave me the phone number and suggested I give him a call. Could it be as simple as that?

We thought it would be fun to ring him and ask about a drum lesson. We hadn't thought of this before now but it seemed appropriate as we were in the process of recording the tribute album back home.

Pete and I debated briefly who should ring and what we should say, but as we were looking for a drum lesson the task was clearly mine. I was a bit nervous because I didn't know how he would react. But this guy was the drummer in Max Webster and a personal hero, so it was well worth the try. To be honest we were a bit surprised that his actual telephone number was in the public domain and so easily accessible. If truth be known we didn't really think he would answer anyway. Wrong!!

I rang the number from Jimmy's landline. We didn't think Jimmy would mind and in hindsight it's a good job we did as Gary rang back on the number later!

The Call (It took a while to answer)

Gary - Hello? (Not in the most welcoming voice)

Mick - Is that Gary McCracken?

Gary - Yes.

Mick - You're not going to believe this, but we are a couple of guys from England, we are massive Max Webster fans and we are currently in the process of recording a Max Webster tribute album. I'm the drummer and it would be great if I could have a lesson off you? (I recall that once I got into my introduction I spoke with more confidence and perhaps a little bit of humour as well, this was a strange situation!)

Gary - It'll be 40 bucks.

(The thing that stood out most was the gap between this statement and the way in which he said it – a bit abrupt. But from his position you can understand why. This may have seemed really odd, and perhaps someone taking the piss? I wonder if that had happened to him before?)

After a very slight delay.

Mick - Yes, that's no problem. Money isn't an issue, to be honest we are just very keen to meet you.

(I might have said that we'd already met Kim Mitchell and even Martin Popoff)

I explained where we were staying and that it might take us a couple of hours to get there, but we would hire a car and come down to see him. I asked what was a good time to meet and we agreed on Wednesday at 3.00pm.

He gave me his address, which I hurriedly jotted down, and once again confirmed that we were genuine, we would definitely turn up and were really looking forward to meeting him. I may even have mentioned that one of the tracks I was keen to work with him on was 'April in Toledo'. There are some tricky bits.

During our brief conversation, he definitely mellowed, but there was still, perhaps understandably an air of suspicion. Had there been the option for me to pay in advance, I definitely would have done so to help dispel his suspicion. I reconfirmed the day, time and venue with him and said goodbye.

Pete and I just laughed when I told him what had just happened and what had been said. Then it dawned on us that we were actually going to meet Gary McCracken – and I was going to get a lesson from the master. We started to look forward very much to this experience and began to plan how we'd get there.

About 10 minutes later, Gary rang back and Pete picked up the phone.

Back to me then!

All of a sudden, the telephone rang. Not thinking anything of it, I answered.

"Hello? Jim Hallam's phone!" A moment of silence, then:

"Hi. It's Gary McCracken. Have you just rung me?"
"Well, I didn't but you spoke to my friend Mick Wilson."

"Yeah! That's right. About a drum lesson. Is he really wanting a drum lesson?"

Slightly confused, I replied "Oh definitely, we're both fans of yours and he definitely wants a lesson. He's a drummer. He's here actually, if you want to speak to him?"

"No! No! That's OK. As long as he's going to turn up?"

"Oh definitely." I replied. "We'll definitely be there. We can't wait."

"Ok! See you then."

And with that, the Great Gary McCracken hung up.

Mick and I looked at each other, then burst out laughing. It all seemed slightly surreal. Obviously, Mr McCracken 125 miles away in Sarnia, Ontario, was asking himself the same question Kim Mitchel had asked us whilst in the Alert offices, 'Why?" Strange times.

A few years earlier, I had got to know the rock biographer and critic Martin Popoff, author of books on Rush, Judas Priest, Blue Oyster Cult, UFO, Deep Purple etc. and Heavy Metal in general. He had new offices located in downtown Toronto, and I had arranged to meet him there.

Prior to visiting Martin, we called at the Hard Rock Cafe in time to coincide with Kim's arrival for his daily Q107 broadcast. Kim remembered us and went out of his way to give us as much time as possible. This time, I managed to conduct myself in a far more articulate manner, even making some sense, for the most part. Kim was genuinely pleased to see us, although he was still slightly bewildered that the Max tribute in England was still in existence.

We asked him how the recent Max Webster reunion for Q107 had gone. He surprised us by saying that a DVD of the show was being prepared for imminent release. Mick and I immediately began to salivate with anticipation.

We told him we would keep our eyes open for its release and couldn't wait to buy it. "Oh, that's ok, we'll send you free copies when it's ready." Said Kim, casually and graciously.

As we prepared to take our leave, we informed him of our imminent meeting with Martin Popoff. Kim asked us to thank Martin on his behalf for his great review for the album 'Ain't life Amazing' as he had really appreciated it. Popoff's review of the album had been very positive, unlike his 'shocking, scathing and totally undeserved review of the album 'Rockland' years earlier. Kim was very angered by the review at the time. Clearly, he'd now moved beyond it.

Saying our farewells, Kim waved us off and we began to make our way to the meeting with Martin Popoff.

~~~~~~~~~~~~~~~~

Martin's office was crammed full of records and memorabilia, a record collector's paradise. He showed us around and played us a few oddities. Mick gave him a gift of Oxym's single in a picture bag, which he was thrilled with.

We knew that Max Webster were Martin's all-time favourite Canadian band. We told him that we had just met Kim Mitchell and that, in the morning, we were driving to Sarnia to meet Gary McCracken. He asked us if we would do him the small favour of taking a number of Max Webster record sleeves with us for Gary to sign. In return, he attempted to contact Pye Dubois, who was a neighbour of his living on Danforth Avenue. We nearly fell through the floor. Surely this couldn't happen. First Kim Mitchell, then Gary McCracken and now Pye Dubois? Three giants of the rock fraternity? Never!

We were right. Never! Martin couldn't get a hold of Pye so, unfortunately, we never got to meet the world's greatest lyricist. Despite that disappointment, the trip was turning out to be a fantastic journey. A research, fact finding mission after all. See... we didn't throw our wives a tall story in the end!

Saying our goodbyes to Martin and promising we would return the album sleeves, safe and signed, we began the short walk along Yonge Street towards the city centre for our return journey to Cambridge and Kitchener.

During this trip the Gods definitely must have been looking down on us. I vaguely knew where we were as we walked along but I was incredibly surprised and pleased to stumble upon the retail outlet for Six Shooter Records, the home of, amongst others, the Rheostatics. Persuading Mick to give me a moment I entered the store.

I passed the time of day with the shop staff for a while, enquiring if there were any new products from the Rheostatics or individual members. Disappointed to hear that there was nothing imminent, I thanked them and turned to leave the store. As I was walking, a small poster caught my eye. It was an advertisement for Martin Tielli of the Rheostatics, who would be performing at the Starlight club in Waterloo tomorrow evening. I was amazed, Martin Tielli, possibly my second favourite Canadian singer, and at Waterloo, which was only a few miles from where we were staying in Cambridge.

Despite already having too much to do, there was no way I was going to miss this once in a lifetime opportunity. Re-joining Mick on Yonge Street, I told him that I would be going to see Martin Tielli after we had got back from Sarnia tomorrow evening, just before we drove to Rick's cottage at around five in the morning. See what I meant? A two-week vacation and everything happening in a two-day period. Mental!

The following morning, having been loaned a car from Jimmy's wonderful wife Val, we set off on the 200-mile round trip to Sarnia, Ontario, the birth place of the mighty Max Webster. It was a fairly quiet and uneventful drive during which we chatted and debated around our favourite Max Webster and Kim Mitchell tracks and we undoubtedly wondered to ourselves and out loud, whether Gary would actually be there when we arrived. Whatever we were chatting about and thinking, the journey passed quickly.

Mick's drum lesson, for forty bucks, was scheduled for around three in the afternoon and we arrived with about an hour to spare. We located the premises where the drum lesson was to take place. Parking the car, we went to get some lunch before meeting Gary.

As we returned, we noticed someone amongst some nearby trees, he seemed to be hiding himself. As we got nearer, this person slowly emerged from the shadows and approached us. Although much older than any photographs we had seen, Mick instantly recognised him as Gary McCracken, one of the world's greatest drummers.

He had obviously been concealing himself from view but, to this day I have no idea why. Perhaps he was still unsure whether we were genuine? We greeted him with great enthusiasm but I think it took him a little longer to be comfortable with these two babbling chaps from England.

He invited us inside to an apartment which was clearly set up for drum lessons but was decorated with Max Webster memorabilia including a 'Max Webster Road' sign and a photo of him with Neil Peart. We were sure to include that in the phots we took with Gary later on.

McCracken was a wondrous joy to encounter. He is so enthusiastic about Max Webster's achievements during their all too brief existence, and so he should be! He regaled us with tale after tale of his time with Max, on the road and in the studio. It was a wonderful privilege to be in his company.

A particularly wondrous story was of the night he had been playing with a local band in a "dive" in Sarnia. His friends were in the west promoting their debut album, '*Max Webster*'. Gary was pleased for his pals, but also envious of their success. Whilst at the club, Gary received a call from Kim Mitchell, telling him that things weren't working out with Paul Kearsey (Max's original drummer) and how would Gary feel about completing the tour and joining Max Webster. Needless to say, he was on the next plane and never looked back. Superb!

Mick's 'drum lesson' was around 20 minutes of him being blown away by Gary playing parts of Max Webster songs on an electronic drum kit. Mick graciously conceded to Gary that he, indeed, was unable to play 'The Party', which brought a knowing satisfactory smile to Mr McCracken's face. Of course he couldn't!

As we were rehearsing our band 'The Universal Juveniles' back home, Mick had particular areas of the songs that he had found difficult. After the lesson, the conversation turned into a discussion about Max Webster and Gary's drumming style which, to be honest, was just what we were after and well worth the forty bucks! We were shown some excellent memorabilia, and gold discs for 'High Class in Borrowed Shoes' and 'A Million Vacations' etc. All mind blowing! We were also shown a sneak preview of the forthcoming Max Webster DVD. The footage of 'The Party' naturally looked amazing and we couldn't wait to see the finished product. Unfortunately, Gary said they needed a six figure sum to get the project completed. Sadly, we are still waiting for its release. Well done the Canadian Music Industry, once more!

What a day! The meeting was over way too soon but I think Gary had other appointments that day. As we made the long journey back to Kitchener, Mick was on cloud nine, unable to believe what had just taken place. We did wonder though, what the world record is for the longest distance travelled for a 'drum lesson'? It may not be the 130 miles or so from Kitchener to Sarnia, but it may very well be the 3,545 miles from Mick's home town of Accrington, Lancashire to Sarnia, Ontario!

We had picked up a couple of copies of Gary's solo CD, 'Audioscapes', and played it in the car during the journey. The CD was never really designed for a commercial release, but it is interesting!

The long day continued when we got back to Kitchener as, that evening, we went to see Martin Tielli perform at the Starlight club. Tielli was magnificent! A sublime performance, which lasted almost three hours. Mick was mortified as he saw any chance of sleep before our journey to Rick's trailer in Port Severn slip away. The only bright spot for Mick was when Tielli segued from the track 'Ship of Fire' into a weird version of Max Webster's 'Gravity'. A superb moment. And one which Mick, fortunately, managed to wake up for..

The rest of the holiday passed by in a manic blur. The time at the trailer, which included seeing the B52s in concert, was good but, to be honest, I was absolutely exhausted and never really got into the right frame of mind to enjoy its magnificent isolation. The B52s were ok, but no great shakes really.

After the trailer park, and back in Toronto, we managed to crowbar in a Toronto FC game and see the Argonauts get trounced once again. All on the same day. I don't know how we managed to stay upright, but it was all good fun.

We finally reached the end of the holiday, completely wiped out but exhilarated. After all of our encounters and experiences, we couldn't wait to get back to putting the finishing touches to the rehearsals for The Universal Juveniles album. We still had three tracks to agree on but, after our adventures, we thought we had them in the bag.

After years of cultivation and preparation it was finally time to complete 'this dream'!

climbing the cloud

By the time we reconvened with The Universal Juveniles, we had the song selections for the album completed. Inspired by Kim's performance and after meeting its author, Gary McCracken, Mick wanted to include 'A Million Vacations' into the running order. I didn't have a problem with this and it opened up new possibilities for us.

At first, the project was going to purely concentrate on the writing genius of Mitchell and Dubois but, as it was a Max Webster tribute, including the compositions of other members made perfect sense. In light of this, I suggested the Terry Watkinson song 'Blowing the Blues Away'. With our own composition already under way, courtesy of Baz, who'd been toying with a few ideas whilst Mick and I had been away, this just left one song to be decided on.

Looking at the songs, it was apparent that this wasn't your average Max Webster song selection. There were definitely some 'oddities' amongst them. We liked this approach and, for the tenth track, I suggested that I go away and compose an a capella version of 'Diamonds Diamonds' to complete the wildly varied selection. With all choices agreed upon, we felt a renewed sense of purpose.

Baz came up with some terrific ideas for our original song. With no lyrics written yet, Baz, myself and Mick arranged the musical sections of the song into some semblance of order. When we were more or less happy with the arrangement, I began to write the lyrics.

The song went through a number of changes over the next few weeks. It originally began life as using snippets of existing Pye Dubois lyrics but I was never really satisfied with what emerged. In the end, and this is no word of a lie, I dreamt the whole song in one night. I woke up, rushed toward a pen and paper, and wrote the whole thing down. With only one or two later alterations, the song was complete.

We adjusted Baz's arrangement for some of the lyrics to fit in and work better and, voila! The song, '(Higher than the moon) Caught in The Web', was born.

For the a capella version of 'Diamonds Diamonds' I contacted a dear friend of mine, David Cook, who had an eight-track home studio at his disposal which, if required, could be doubled to sixteen tracks. It was just what I needed. Cheap (free actually!) and convenient.

Unfortunately, Dave, a life-long friend of the family, had recently been diagnosed with lung cancer. Despite being very ill at the time, due to the disease and his treatment, he was still happy to help me record the song. That was typical of Dave, he was always ready to go out of his way to help others, always there for you. A musician himself, he just loved the whole creative process and I believe he thoroughly enjoyed our recording session.

Sadly, Dave succumbed to the cancer and passed away in early 2010. He'll be sorely missed by everyone who was fortunate enough to have known him. I am so pleased and grateful that he played such an integral part in this story.

Dave recorded sixteen of my vocal tracks for a demo to take to the band. The idea being that, at some point in the future, they would learn their parts to be ready for recording in the studio.

Rehearsals nearly complete, we set a date for the studio. We chose the company Studio Studio in Lancashire. Myself and Wilko had used the studio previously, it was where I recorded part of the Electricgarden CD, 'Tango of Life'. The engineer and owner of the company, Pete Troughton, was a very good, fast and sympathetic engineer and we felt that he would be perfect for the sessions.

Time ran out on us a little by the time recording began. We hadn't had time to rehearse the 'Diamonds Diamonds' section, so it was agreed that the demo version would be used. Not as a full song, but as part of another. As time went on, we chose to include it into our version of 'Blue River Liquor Shine'.

The recording, plus the mixing, was completed over twelve days and it all went fantastically well. The band excelled themselves. Around eighty percent of the tracks were first takes, which is incredible when you think about the complexity of these songs. We were all incredibly pleased with the end results and in particular, the sequencing of the album.

At first the album was to be called 'Music To Thin The Thickness Of Your Skin' but, at the eleventh hour, and thanks to Mick, that title was changed to the much improved 'Climbing A Cloud'.

Opening with 'Coming off The Moon', it then goes straight into 'A Million Vacations' (complete with car horn sound effects) and is quickly followed by 'April in Toledo'. The mood then shifts to the country feel of 'Blowing the Blues Away'. We extended the ending of this song, giving Wilko a chance for a long guitar solo. As the solo begins to fade, we inserted the sound of surf and seagulls as homage to the song 'Hawaii'. We even included the sound of Mick yawning, as Kim does at the beginning of that same song.

Track five is our much more acoustic version of 'Words to Words', which is followed by my favourite piece of the album, 'Distressed'.

Next up is our own composition, '(Higher than the moon) Caught In The Web', which I am pleased to say stands up pretty well against the other classic rock giants.

The album closes with two more songs from the Universal Juveniles album. First is our extended version of 'Blue River Liquor Shine'. We extend the ending here, so that we can include a few more nods and winks to max's past. Firstly, as the song begins its long, extended fade-out we introduce the sound of a theatre crowd, as a nod to the opening of 'The Party'. After this, our a capella version of 'Diamonds Diamonds' briefly fades in and out. As it begins to fade away, we insert our own version of a coin being tossed as in the song 'Gravity'.

All these subliminal touches were actually quite painstaking to produce, but all were tremendous fun and I hope they come across as well-intentioned as they were meant to be.

The album closes with the bands collective favourite, 'Check'. A very hard track to follow, so suitably chosen as the last number.

And there you have it. 'Climbing a Cloud'. A Tribute to Max Webster by 'The Universal Juveniles'. A staggering nine years after its conception the recording was complete.

It was now time to think about its presentation and release. Time to find out what the world would make of our efforts. Perhaps we would even take the Juveniles out to meet the public face to face in a live setting? That had never been our intention, but?

Maybe, it was time to 'Rock That Rhyme'!

that'r the rtory!

We were all absolutely thrilled with the recordings we had achieved at Studio Studio. As I've said, everyone had been at the top of their game, including the engineer and Studio owner Pete Troughton.

Although Pete finished the recording sessions by adding just a touch of compression to the tracks, making it all sound fantastic, Mick and I decided to take the recordings to a company to be 'mastered'. This is a process which is performed on all professional recordings. It's designed to smooth out any high-end sound 'spikes' and low-end distortion, making the record sound as good as possible, whatever sound system the listener may be using. Particularly important for radio broadcast.

We chose a company that sounded just right for our kind of material, and budget. We sent the recordings off to them and waited with baited breath for their return.

After a few days, they sent us back a 'finished' version for our approval. Thankfully, it wasn't the finalised master.

I was absolutely gutted! They had butchered it! Not only was it unlistenable, it was also unrecognisable. I really have no idea what these people were thinking. Had they even listened to what they had done before sending it back to us? Doubtful! It was 39 minutes of 'white noise'. Just a 'swooshing and whooshing' sound. On every track.

I was distraught.

I turned my back on the company at that point. I had no faith in them whatsoever. Mick persevered with them for a time (he has much more patience than I have) and he received and listened to two or three further versions, but they didn't really get any better. Eventually, we scrapped all involvement with the company and took the tapes back to Pete Troughton at Studio Studio.

Pete did the best he could and tried to restore the album back to its former glory. To me though, it never sounded as good as it had originally. It's a little 'harsh' sounding and has lost some warmth. But, after nine years, we had what we had.

When it came to the packaging and presentation of the CD, we had a number of ideas. Whilst in the studio we had taken quite a few photographs of the band, both performing and posing. I asked my brother, Jim, who's quite a talented artist, if he could create a painting for use as the possible cover for the album. After a few, abstract, guidelines from myself, he came up with the wonderful painting 'Welcome to Sarnia'.

Also, Mick's lovely 14-year-old daughter Hannah, had been designing a band 'logo' for us. So, we had a lot of ideas to play with and choose from. In the end, we went with using almost all of it.

The painting 'Welcome to Sarnia' ended up on the rear of the booklet. Hannah's logo went in the CD tray, and the band photographs were displayed within the pages, along with a photo of our collective Max Webster memorabilia.

One of the bands 'posing' photos was our take on the 'High Class in Borrowed Shoes' album cover, this image was reimagined into an illustration by an artist Mick had stumbled across whilst on vacation. We all liked the image so much that we decided that that would be the cover. So, overall, a plethora of Max related thought went into the presentation. Moon references abound.

The album was finally released in 2010 on our own 'Fanthumb' label, a terrible pun on Anthem records, the home of both Max Webster and Rush, and Kim Mitchell's mythological 'long thumb'.

Next! We decided to launch and promote the album by performing live in front of the public. We chose to keep it all rather low key, and performed on three separate occasions before private audiences, Mick's 50th birthday celebrations being one of those.

We played twice in my hometown of Clitheroe and at Mick's birthday party in his hometown of Accrington. We gave them, 'Coming off the Moon', 'A Million Vacations', 'Blue River Liqueur Shine', 'Check', our own '(Higher than the Moon) Caught in the Web', and for good measure (and new for us), 'Night Flights'.

Although we performed pretty well at all three shows, the audience reaction was at best, indifferent. Pearls before swine? Although we sold a few CDs at the venues, we never felt the urge to repeat the shows or take it any further. We did manage to sell quite a few copies on line and to many different parts of the world, including Canada, which I was very pleased about!

Speaking of which, my beautiful wife and I returned to visit our friends in Ontario towards the end of 2010. During the visit, I managed to make a quick visit to the Q107 radio station at the Hard Rock Cafe. I was able to distract Kim Mitchell from his broadcasting long enough to hand him a couple of copies of 'Climbing a Cloud'. We didn't really have time to chat as he was obviously busy. He thanked me though and wished me well, but to be honest, he still just looked a bit bemused by the whole thing. Oh well!

I'm pleased to say 'Climbing a Cloud', hadn't put Kim Mitchell off performing. We saw him play a storming set at Toronto's Bandshell theatre toward the end of our visit. A superb performance which incorporated a lot more Max material than previously. Maybe (subliminally) the Universal Juveniles had an effect on Mr Mitchell!

He had us 'dancing to an old song'.

time to go

Discovering 'The Big Fantasize' (2020)

The Universal Juveniles didn't carry on for much longer after the release of 'Climbing a Cloud', there didn't seem much point as it seemed as though we had completed all we had set out to do. So, with heavy hearts all around, we went our separate ways in early 2011.

Mick and I continued to work together, resurrecting the 'New Wave of British Heavy Metal' band 'Oxym', and in 2016, with all original members of the 1982 line up, we recorded an album of all original material entitled 'Passing Through Gateways'.

We played live a number of times, and I'm so proud to be able to say that our last performance, mine and Mick's last performance anywhere to date, was at Newcastle University, Northumberland, at 'Brofest 4' on a bill supporting Martin Turner of Wishbone Ash fame.

Brofest is an annual festival celebrating the 'New Wave of British Heavy Metal' movement which lasted from around 1978 to 1982. A fantastic day, and a memorable way to bow out of live performing.

As one lifelong obsession of mine began to fade, another began. On 25th October 2015 I became a very proud Grandfather when my darling Granddaughter Clara, entered our world. As I write this, Ann's daughter Kayla, is expecting a boy! At least now I will get to sing the odd lullaby or two.

Just as things were quietening down, in 2020, we were treated with a huge surprise. Ten years after the release of his last album, Kim Mitchell returned to the recording world and presented us with 'The Big Fantasize', his eighth solo studio album, if you don't include the 'Kim Mitchell' EP.

The album found Mitchell in a very laid back, reflective mood. It received mixed reviews from fans and critics, which is a shame. Yes, there are perhaps one or two too many slower numbers on the album, but aged 68 when the album was recorded, maybe he had decided that his 'Rock and Roll' duty was nearing a graceful end? At least recording wise anyway. If that's the case, then nobody can deny he's earned the right.

The album is sublime. The production, by Gregg Wells, reminding me of the period from 'Shakin' like a Human Being' through to 'Aural Fixations' and in particular, the album 'Rockland'.

Once we get beyond the confusing and underwhelming cover for the album, we mostly find Kim in a country music mood. Don't switch off here. Kim Mitchell, and indeed the mighty Max Webster themselves have always had a touch of country in their respective repertoires. Just think of 'Some Folks' from Kim's 'Aural Fixations' or 'Blowing the Blues Away' from as far back as Max's debut.

A large cast of players and composers, old and new, contributed to making this, rather short, but worthy addition, to Mitchell's career.

It's mostly an acoustic guitar album throughout, and opening track, 'Red Horizon' makes us aware of this straight off. An old-fashioned campfire song, Mitchell accompanied by an 'orchestra'! The song is nice enough but, for these ears, the orchestral accompaniment smothers it making it far too 'syrupy'. Perhaps it would have been more effective if it had just been Kim and his superb acoustic guitar work.

'2up2Bdown' is much more like it! If this had been released as a single in 1984-89 it would have been another sure-fire summer radio hit! A fist pumping, feel good, upbeat anthem.

'Summer Lovers Autumn Wine' is simply gorgeous. Very reminiscent of material from 'Rockland'. Although piano is very prominent throughout, it's a tasteful addition to a sorrowful song of lost love and heartache. Thankfully, an orchestra is nowhere to be seen. Superb!

Next up? 'Wishes'. Although it definitely stays in keeping with the overall theme and style of the album, for me, it's one of Mitchell's weaker tracks. A fairly simple love song. The lyrics are perhaps, a little too 'literal'. It's obviously heartfelt and sincere, as most of this album is, but seems a little 'throwaway'?

'Georgian Bay' puts the album back on the right track. A much needed 'up tempo' number. A fun-filled, bar room boogie stomp! Conjuring up memories of 'Lemon Wedge' from 'Itch'. Prominent piano again dominates, to the detriment of guitar, which appears totally absent from this track. How strange! Kim Mitchell, again, displaying his, eclectic, versatility. Totally enjoyable!

The album's centrepiece is surely 'Best I Never Had'. A gutsy, New Orleans, sweat soaked, southern raunch! Fantastic! The emotion, here, in both Mitchell's vocals and guitar is palpable. Simply a great rock song, worthy of a place on any of his previous albums.

Next up, 'Montgomery'. A strong, nicely arranged, country song in the vein of early Eagles. Not too dissimilar to 'Wishes' but better. Stronger, both lyrically and musically. Nothing too outstanding, but solid!

'Old Marriage Waltz' would definitely be a track that split opinion amongst fans, with most, I suspect, not really buying into its over sentimentality. It's quite clever in its arrangement, but, even though I quite like it, I'm not sure it's a number that fits well amongst Mitchell's repertoire. I prefer it to 'Wishes' though, and one or two others from past albums.

The album ends with 'Time to Stay'. No real attempt to up the tempo or change the mood of the album here. Although the feel is a little more 'funky' than anything else on the album. Quite atmospheric and a real grower. If the nine tracks here are all Kim had to choose from, then 'Time to Stay' is probably the best choice to end with.

A mixed bag, really, but at least the album is consistent throughout with its themes and style. Which I like.

So! There you have it. Could this be Kim Mitchell's final album? He's now in his seventies, so it's possible. Obviously, I hope this isn't the case. If there is to be another album in the future, I also hope for a 'slightly' heavier offering, as he can still rock like a mother! as evidenced by the four live bonus tracks affixed to 'The Big Fantasize'. These tracks just knock you off your feet. What a band! Stunning performances, including the live rarity of Max's 'Paradise Skies'. Another, full length, live album from Kim Mitchell is long overdue.

That, more or less, brings the story to a close. Except...

On an extremely sad note to end, Baz Oldale, our very gifted guitarist from The Universal Juveniles, and a dear friend, succumbed to cancer in 2016. Whenever I listen to 'Climbing a Cloud: A Tribute to Max Webster', it almost feels like a tribute to Baz and brings back only good memories of our time with him.

So. That's the story! It's time to go! I'll raise a glass to Baz and all who played their part in this journey. Especially Kim Mitchell, without whose 'talent', 'creativity', 'stubbornness', 'Drive and Desire', the world, and my world in particular, would be a much less exciting place to be.

Cheers!

Now, where did I leave my cigarettes and matches?

afterword

The main body of this book was written in 2010. At that time, particularly in little ol' Lancashire in England, there was very little information available regarding the formative years of Max Webster and the origins of their songs and albums.

In 2023 that was all corrected with the release of the wonderful 'tome' 'Max Webster High Class', the definitive history of the band by Bob Wegner.

In my naiveté, I could only write my personal thoughts and summations in relation to Max Webster's and Kim Mitchell's work. Bob Wegner's book tells it all as it really was.

I have chosen not to rectify any assumptions that were made on my part, as I wanted the story to remain in the spirit of the time it was written. 2010 also being the year that the album 'Climbing a Cloud. A Tribute to Max Webster' by The Universal Juveniles, was released.

Peter Joe Hulmes.

acknowledgments

There are so many people whom I would like to acknowledge and thank, but I'll try to keep it brief.

First, for their inspiration, I would like to thank Martin Popoff and Dave Bidini, whose writings were the catalyst for this project. Particularly Dave Bidini's wonderful book, 'On A Cold Road'. For those who haven't read this book, shame on you! It's essential reading.

I would also like to thank all members of the magnificent Max Webster and the Kim Mitchell Band both past and present.

Special thanks go out to the Canadian Crew, without whom none of this story would have been possible. They are: Rick and Gail Beckett, Winston Beckett R.I.P. Jimmy Hallam and Valerie Ryan, David 'Mitch' Mitchell (he of two chins), Stan, Penny and Brad, Donny, Donny, Bonny and Lorne (don't ask), the two Marks and everyone else in the Great White North who I am proud to call a friend. Thank you!

The members of The Universal Juveniles, especially my partner in crime Mick Wilson, and those who played a part in the long process at some stage or other. All deserve my thanks. All friends and family, especially my brother Jim for the wonderful cover painting (Welcome To Sarnia) for the album 'Climbing a Cloud: A Tribute to Max Webster'.

Thanks also to Mick Wilson and James Hallam for providing the photographs, as well as Tom Berry for the photo with Kim in the Alert Music office.

Special thanks to Bob Holt for never forgetting this book existed for over ten years and encouraging me to blow the dust off it and get it finished. Along with his commitment, encouragement, and hard work, editing the manuscript and formatting it for publication.

And last, but by no means least, my gorgeous wife Ann and her two beautiful daughters, Tanita and Kayla, for support, love and invaluable input, and my darling daughter, Leigh-Anne, for her support and help in the finishing touches and saving the project from total disaster.

My love and gratitude to you all.

Peter Joe Hulmes.

links

http://www.kimmitchell.ca
Current website for the living God that is Kim Mitchell. Links to news, videos and tour dates when available.

https://bobwegner.ca/
Bob Wegner, the author of the amazing book High Class is also an accomplished guitarist who has toured the world.

https://highclassmax.com/
The link to preview and order Bob Wegner's Max Webster book.

https://www.maxwebsterlive.ca/
Another Bob Wegner website that presents all the available information on Max Webster's live performances.

https://www.maxwebster.ca/
A fan developed and managed website with a broad variety of Max Webster information.

For a copy of The Universal Juveniles CD Climbing a Cloud - A Tribute to Max Webster, please contact:
mike@universaljuveniles.co.uk

For feedback or to contact the author email:
unijuve@yahoo.com

www.ingramcontent.com/pod-product-compliance
Lightning Source LLC
Chambersburg PA
CBHW072146290526
45794CB00004B/1434